INTRODUCING
ISSUES WITH
OPPOSING
VIEWPOINTS®

# Energy
# Alternatives

INTRODUCING
ISSUES WITH
OPPOSING
VIEWPOINTS®

# Energy
# Alternatives

Other books in the Introducing Issues
with Opposing Viewpoints series:

AIDS
Alcohol
Animal Rights
Civil Liberties
Cloning
The Death Penalty
The Environment
Gangs
Gay Marriage
Genetic Engineering
Islam
Smoking
Terrorism
UFOs

# INTRODUCING ISSUES WITH OPPOSING VIEWPOINTS®

# Energy Alternatives

Laura K. Egendorf, *Book Editor*

Bonnie Szumski, *Publisher, Series Editor*
Helen Cothran, *Managing Editor*

**GREENHAVEN PRESS**
*An imprint of Thomson Gale, a part of The Thomson Corporation*

THOMSON

GALE

Detroit • New York • San Francisco • San Diego • New Haven, Conn. • Waterville, Maine • London • Munich

**LIBRARY OF CONGRESS CATALOGING-IN-PUBLICATION DATA**

Energy alternatives / Laura K. Egendorf, book editor.
    p. cm. — (Introducing issues with opposing viewpoints)
    Includes bibliographical references and index.
    ISBN 0-7377-3458-2 (lib : alk. paper)
    1. Power resources. 2. Renewable energy sources. I. Egendorf, Laura K., 1973– .
II. Series.
    TJ163.2E454 2006
    333.79—dc22
                                                        2005055143

Printed in the United States of America

# Contents

## Chapter 3: Should Alternatives to Gasoline-Powered Vehicles Be Pursued?

# Foreword

Indulging in a wide spectrum of ideas, beliefs, and perspectives is a critical cornerstone of democracy. After all, it is often debates over differences of opinion, such as whether to legalize abortion, how to treat prisoners, or when to enact the death penalty, that shape our society and drive it forward. Such diversity of thought is frequently regarded as the hallmark of a healthy and civilized culture. As the Reverend Clifford Schutjer of the First Congregational Church in Mansfield, Ohio, declared in a 2001 sermon, "Surrounding oneself with only like-minded people, restricting what we listen to or read only to what we find agreeable is irresponsible. Refusing to entertain doubts once we make up our minds is a subtle but deadly form of arrogance." With this advice in mind, Introducing Issues with Opposing Viewpoints books aim to open readers' minds to the critically divergent views that comprise our world's most important debates.

Introducing Issues with Opposing Viewpoints simplifies for students the enormous and often overwhelming mass of material now available via print and electronic media. Collected in every volume is an array of opinions that captures the essence of a particular controversy or topic. Introducing Issues with Opposing Viewpoints books embody the spirit of nineteenth-century journalist Charles A. Dana's axiom: "Fight for your opinions, but do not believe that they contain the whole truth, or the only truth." Absorbing such contrasting opinions teaches students to analyze the strength of an argument and compare it to its opposition. From this process readers can inform and strengthen their own opinions, or be exposed to new information that will change their minds. Introducing Issues with Opposing Viewpoints is a mosaic of different voices. The authors are statesmen, pundits, academics, journalists, corporations, and ordinary people who have felt compelled to share their experiences and ideas in a public forum. Their words have been collected from newspapers, journals, books, speeches, interviews, and the Internet, the fastest growing body of opinionated material in the world.

Introducing Issues with Opposing Viewpoints shares many of the well-known features of its critically acclaimed parent series, Opposing Viewpoints. The articles are presented in a pro/con format, allowing readers to absorb divergent perspectives side by side. Active reading questions preface each viewpoint, requiring the student to approach the material thoughtfully and carefully. Useful charts, graphs, and cartoons supplement each article. A thorough introduction provides readers with crucial background on an issue. An annotated bibliography points the reader toward articles, books, and Web sites that contain additional information on the topic. An appendix of organizations to contact contains a wide variety of charities, nonprofit organizations, political groups, and private enterprises that each hold a position on the issue at hand. Finally, a comprehensive index allows readers to locate content quickly and efficiently.

Introducing Issues with Opposing Viewpoints is also significantly different from Opposing Viewpoints. As the series title implies, its presentation will help introduce students to the concept of opposing viewpoints, and learn to use this material to aid in critical writing and debate. The series' four-color, accessible format makes the books attractive and inviting to readers of all levels. In addition, each viewpoint has been carefully edited to maximize a reader's understanding of the content. Short but thorough viewpoints capture the essence of an argument. A substantial, thought-provoking essay question placed at the end of each viewpoint asks the student to further investigate the issues raised in the viewpoint, compare and contrast two authors' arguments, or consider how one might go about forming an opinion on the topic at hand. Each viewpoint contains sidebars that include at-a-glance information and handy statistics. A Facts About section located in the back of the book further supplies students with relevant facts and figures.

Following in the tradition of the Opposing Viewpoints series, Greenhaven Press continues to provide readers with invaluable exposure to the controversial issues that shape our world. As John Stuart Mill once wrote: "The only way in which a human being can make some approach to knowing the whole of a subject is by hearing what can be said about it by persons of every variety of opinion and studying all modes in which it can be looked at by every character of mind. No wise man ever acquired his wisdom in any mode but this." It is to this principle that Introducing Issues with Opposing Viewpoints books are dedicated.

# Introduction

Throughout history, people have investigated alternative energies only when there is a crisis or interruption with their primary fuel source. For example, in the nineteenth century during the height of the Industrial Revolution, numerous scientists and inventors feared that the supply of coal would run out. At the time, coal was the primary fuel source for machines and engines. In the panic over a possible coal shortage, several people tried to develop engines that ran on alternative energy sources, such as solar power. Most of these efforts were too impractical and expensive to be of much use, however. Coal was soon replaced by oil, and efforts toward alternative energies were largely abandoned. But more than a century later, high fuel costs and dwindling supplies have led people to again investigate whether alternative energy sources can replace or supplement their primary fuel source.

The first time alternatives to oil were earnestly explored was after the energy crisis of 1973. The crisis began when the Arab members of the Organization of Petroleum Exporting Countries (OPEC) announced that they would stop sending oil to the United States as retribution for supporting Israel against Egypt in the Yom Kippur War. Although the embargo lasted only five months, it caused the cost of oil to quadruple (from $3 per barrel to $12 per barrel), leading to oil shortages in the United States and long lines at gas stations.

Hoping to prevent similar problems should another embargo occur, the federal government turned its attention toward energy alternatives. In 1975 Congress created the Energy Research and Development Administration, an agency that supported scientific research into energy alternatives. Another step taken by Congress was the passage of the National Energy Act of 1978, which featured a series of taxes geared to encourage the transition to alternative fuels. The government also introduced tax incentives to spur the development of energy alternatives.

These efforts led to a rebirth of alternative energy. Professor of technology Charles Smith explains, "During the 1970s . . . mechanical solar power—along with its space-age, electricity-producing sibling photovoltaics, as well as other renewable sources such as wind

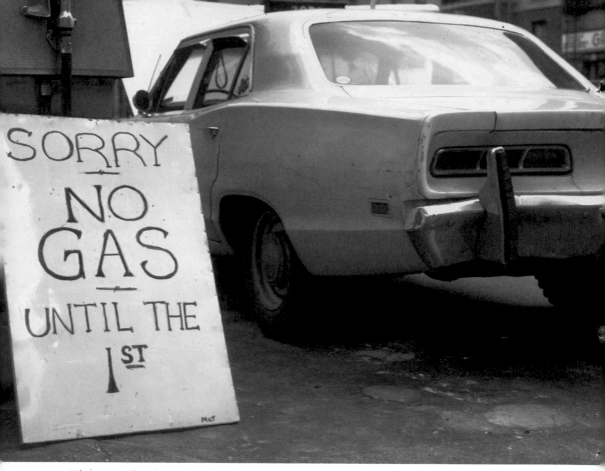

*The 1973 oil embargo by oil-producing Arab nations led to severe shortages at gas stations across the United States.*

power—underwent a revival."[1] At the peak of the energy crisis, fifty American companies manufactured wind turbines; according to the Iowa Energy Center, a single machine could provide enough power for seven hundred homes. Engineers also worked on creating more efficient solar collectors, devices that intercept solar radiation and convert it into thermal energy and electricity.

For the better part of a decade it appeared that energy alternatives had made permanent inroads into the United States. But by the mid-1980s, America had returned to an oil-dominated economy. Much of this was due to the change in presidential administrations, from Democrat Jimmy Carter to Republican Ronald Reagan, who did not support alternative energy. In 1979 the federal renewable research and development budget was $856.9 million; by 1990 it had been cut to less than 10 percent of that amount. The impact was significant. In 1991 the leading producer of solar-generated electricity filed for bankruptcy, in large part because it had lost almost all government support. By 1997 fewer than a dozen manufacturers produced wind turbines. Oil prices also led to a move away from energy alternatives. Prices fell nearly in half by the late 1980s, to less than $10 per barrel, making oil significantly more affordable and convenient than other energy sources.

With a few exceptions, such as the electric cars that briefly garnered attention in the mid-1990s, alternative energy was largely ignored until the twenty-first century. It was then that debate reemerged as to whether dependence on foreign oil had become too problematic and if oil production was nearing its peak. Adding to the debate were allegations of global warming, which environmentalists believe is caused by the burning of fossil fuels such as oil. Furthermore, rising oil costs

*In the aftermath of the 1973 energy crisis, American policy makers began to seriously explore the potential of energy alternatives such as wind power.*

and political instability in oil-producing nations also made people wonder whether relying so heavily on oil was the best idea. All of these issues sparked a renewed interest in energy alternatives.

Though alternative energy has become more popular in recent years, it is not close to replacing oil and other fossil fuels. As of 2005, alternative fuels still make up barely 1 percent of U.S. energy use and face problems expanding. As was the case during the Industrial Revolution, cost and practicality remain issues. The government, however, is again encouraging consumers to use energy alternatives; the Energy Policy Act of 2005 authorized tax incentives for building residential solar power systems, purchasing alternative-fuel cars, and using renewable electricity sources such as wind and biomass. As President George W.

*Accompanied by a technician, President Bush tours the first hydrogen fueling station in the United States, located in Washington, D.C.*

Bush explained when he signed the bill into law, "By developing these innovative technologies, we can keep the lights running while protecting the environment and using energy produced right here at home."[2]

Whether the current interest in alternative energy sources will last longer than in the past or spur more permanent changes in energy consumption remains to be seen. The authors in *Introducing Issues with Opposing Viewpoints: Energy Alternatives* explore the status of alternative fuels in the following chapters: Are Alternative Energy Sources Necessary? Are Alternative Energy Sources Viable? Should Alternatives to Gasoline-Powered Vehicles Be Pursued? The viewpoints in this volume suggest that the debate over alternative energy is not likely to be settled any time soon.

## Notes

1. Charles Smith, "History of Solar Energy," *Technology Review*, July 1995.

2. President George W. Bush, remarks at Sandia National Laboratory in Albuquerque, New Mexico, August 8, 2005.

# Chapter 1

# Are Alternative Energy Sources Necessary?

Most Americans rely on fossil fuel–powered automobiles for transportation.

**Viewpoint**
**1**

# The World Is Facing an Energy Crisis

### James Howard Kunstler

*"We face the end of the cheap-fossil-fuel era."*

The world is running out of oil, James Howard Kunstler argues in the following viewpoint. Because Americans rely on oil in all aspects of their life, Kunstler predicts the gradual decline in oil production will create a vastly different society. He also believes that the problems created by the looming oil shortage cannot be solved by using alternative sources of energy.

Kunstler is a columnist who focuses on environmental and economic issues.

**AS YOU READ, CONSIDER THE FOLLOWING QUESTIONS:**

1. According to Kunstler, how many barrels of oil did the United States produce each day in 2004?
2. What do "cornucopians" believe, as explained by the author?
3. What does Kunstler believe is the worst choice made by America in the twentieth century?

James Howard Kunstler, *The Long Emergency*. New York: Atlantic Monthly Press, 2005. Copyright © 2005 by Grove/Atlantic, Inc. Reproduced by permission.

It has been very hard for Americans—lost in dark raptures of non-stop infotainment, recreational shopping and compulsive motoring—to make sense of the gathering forces that will fundamentally alter the terms of everyday life in our technological society. Even after the terrorist attacks of 9/11, America is still sleepwalking into the future. I call this coming time the Long Emergency.

Most immediately we face the end of the cheap-fossil-fuel era. It is no exaggeration to state that reliable supplies of cheap oil and natural gas underlie everything we identify as the necessities of modern life—not to mention all of its comforts and luxuries: central heating, air conditioning, cars, airplanes, electric lights, inexpensive clothing, recorded music, movies, hip-replacement surgery, national defense—you name it.

## The Global Oil-Production Peak

The few Americans who are even aware that there is a gathering global-energy predicament usually misunderstand the core of the argument.

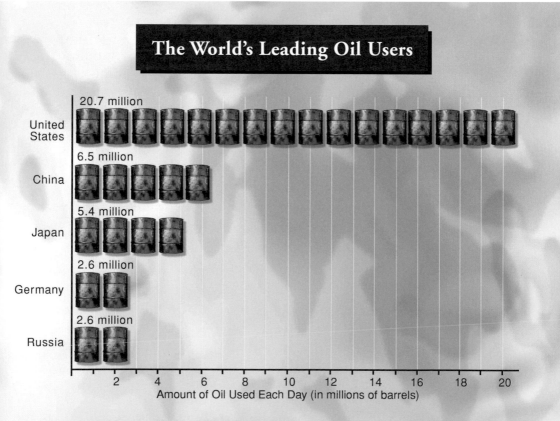

**The World's Leading Oil Users**

United States: 20.7 million

China: 6.5 million

Japan: 5.4 million

Germany: 2.6 million

Russia: 2.6 million

Amount of Oil Used Each Day (in millions of barrels)

Source: Energy Information Administration, 2004.

That argument states that we don't have to run out of oil to start having severe problems with industrial civilization and its dependent systems. We only have to slip over the all-time production peak and begin a slide down the arc of steady depletion.

The term "global oil-production peak" means that a turning point will come when the world produces the most oil it will ever produce in a given year and, after that, yearly production will inexorably decline. It is usually represented graphically in a bell curve. The peak is the top of the curve, the halfway point of the world's all-time total endowment, meaning half the world's oil will be left. That seems like a lot of oil, and it is, but there's a big catch: It's the half that is much more difficult to extract, far more costly to get, of much poorer quality and located mostly in places where the people hate us. A substantial amount of it will never be extracted.

**FAST FACT**

The average American uses 23.4 barrels of oil each year.

The United States passed its own oil peak about 11 million barrels a day—in 1970, and since then production has dropped steadily. In 2004 it ran just above 5 million barrels a day (we get a tad more from natural-gas condensates). Yet we consume roughly 20 million barrels a day now. That means we have to import about two-thirds of our oil, and the ratio will continue to worsen.

## We Are Running Out of Oil

The U.S. peak in 1970 brought on a portentous change in geoeconomic power. Within a few years, foreign producers, chiefly OPEC [Organization of Petroleum Exporting Countries], were setting the price of oil, and this in turn led to the oil crises of the 1970s. In response, frantic development of non-OPEC oil, especially the North Sea fields of England and Norway, essentially saved the West . . . for about two decades. Since 1999, these fields have entered depletion. Meanwhile, worldwide discovery of new oil has steadily declined to insignificant levels in 2003 and 2004.

Some "cornucopians" claim that the Earth has something like a creamy nougat center of "abiotic" [which comes from geological sources and not

*Drilling rigs, such as this one in Kentucky, typically produce little more than one or two barrels of oil per day.*

fossils] oil that will naturally replenish the great oil fields of the world. The facts speak differently. There has been no replacement whatsoever of oil already extracted from the fields of America or any other place.

Now we are faced with the global oil-production peak. The best estimates of when this will actually happen have been somewhere between now and 2010. In 2004, however, after demand from burgeoning China and India shot up, and revelations that Shell Oil wildly misstated its reserves, and Saudi Arabia proved incapable of goosing up its production despite promises to do so, the most knowledgeable experts revised their predictions and now concur that 2005 is apt to be the year of all-time global peak production.

It will change everything about how we live. . . .

## There Will Be Radical Changes to American Life

We will have to accommodate ourselves to fundamentally changed conditions. No combination of alternative fuels will allow us to run American life the way we have been used to running it, or even a substantial fraction of it. The wonders of steady technological progress achieved through the reign of cheap oil have lulled us into a kind of Jiminy Cricket syndrome, leading many Americans to believe that anything we wish for hard enough will come true. These days, even people who ought to know better are wishing ardently for a seamless transition from fossil fuels to their putative replacements. . . .

*The suburban lifestyle of most Americans may become impossible if energy shortages make traveling long distances difficult.*

The Long Emergency will require us to make other arrangements for the way we live in the United States. America is in a special predicament due to a set of unfortunate choices we made as a society in the twentieth century. Perhaps the worst was to let our towns and cities rot away and to replace them with suburbia, which had the additional side effect of trashing a lot of the best farmland in America. Suburbia will come to be regarded as the greatest misallocation of resources in the history of the world. It has a tragic destiny. The psychology of previous investment suggests that we will defend our drive-in utopia long after it has become a terrible liability.

Before long, the suburbs will fail us in practical terms. We made the ongoing development of housing subdivisions, highway strips, fried-food shacks and shopping malls the basis of our economy, and when we have to stop making more of those things, the bottom will fall out.

## A Downscaled Future

The circumstances of the Long Emergency will require us to downscale and re-scale virtually everything we do and how we do it, from the kind of communities we physically inhabit to the way we grow our food to the way we work and trade the products of our work. Our lives will become profoundly and intensely local. Daily life will be far less about mobility and much more about staying where you are. Anything organized on the large scale, whether it is government or a corporate business enterprise such as Wal-Mart, will wither as the cheap energy props that support bigness fall away. The turbulence of the Long Emergency will produce a lot of economic losers, and many of these will be members of an angry and aggrieved former middle class.

**EVALUATING THE AUTHOR'S ARGUMENTS:**

In this viewpoint James Howard Kunstler argues that oil and gas are critical to everyday life. Do you think he exaggerates the role of these fuels? Why or why not?

# The World Is Not Facing an Energy Crisis

**Julie Creswell**

> *"Oil and natural gas are being found in places no one expected and in greater quantities than anticipated just a decade ago."*

In the following viewpoint Julie Creswell examines scientific theories that suggest the planet will never run out of oil. She explains that some scientists believe oil and gas can be found deep within the earth and that the supply of these fuels is constantly replenished. Although other scientists doubt these theories, Creswell points out that other long-standing scientific views have been proven wrong.

Creswell is a regular contributor to *Fortune* magazine, a semiweekly publication that focuses on business and financial issues.

**AS YOU READ, CONSIDER THE FOLLOWING QUESTIONS:**
1. How much oil was produced per day in the White Tiger Field in 2002, according to Creswell?
2. What were the findings of the Siljan Lake project?
3. According to the author, what is Thomas Gold's theory on how oil and natural gas were created?

In the quiet waters off the coast of Vietnam lies an area known as Bach Ho, or White Tiger Field. There, and in the nearby Black Bear and Black Lion fields, exploration companies are drilling more than a mile into solid granite—so-called basement rock—for oil. That's a puzzle: Oil isn't supposed to be found in basement rock, which never rose near the surface of the earth where ancient plants grew and dinosaurs walked. Yet oil is there. [In 2002] the White Tiger Field and nearby areas produced 338,000 barrels per day, and they are estimated to hold about 600 million barrels more.

Oil and natural gas are being found in places no one expected and in greater quantities than anticipated just a decade ago. In the mid-1990s the world's reserves of oil were thought to total about 890 billion barrels. Today reserves stand at 1.1 trillion barrels; the U.S. Geological Survey estimates that continued reserve growth, along with undiscovered resources, could bring world oil estimates to as much as three trillion barrels. "We're finding there are pretty substantial oil reserves in the world," says Tom Ahlbrandt, world energy project chief at the USGS. "New exploration and drilling technologies are making major new discoveries possible."

*A worker at a natural gas drilling rig in Wyoming tightens a section of drilling pipe. New sources of natural gas are being discovered throughout the world.*

*Workers set pipes in place on an oil rig. New drilling technologies have made it possible to tap previously undiscovered oil reserves.*

## Unconventional Theories

The increase in reserve estimates is fueling the offbeat theories of maverick scientists who believe that the expression "fossil fuels" is a misnomer and that the earth contains a virtually endless supply of oil. Their ideas fly in the face of the conventional wisdom that oil and natural gas come from the remains of animals and plants buried millions of years ago. Subterranean heat and pressure, mainstream science says, transformed this organic dreck into coal and oil. Though their theories vary, the upstarts believe instead that wellsprings of oil and gas lie deep within the earth, deeper than most oil companies drill, and that supplies are constantly replenished. "With the White Tiger Field in Vietnam, 90% of the production is coming from basement rock, where there were never any fossils," argues C. Warren Hunt, a geologist in Calgary. "What they've been teaching us in school about oil coming from fossils is wrong."

If true, the theories may mean we can stress less about running out of oil: There's more where that came from! We can also worry less about tensions in the Middle East or other hot spots cutting off our long-term supply. Problem is, most scientists scoff at such theories. Oil companies maintain that even if the rebels are right, the cost of searching for and extracting deep oil is prohibitive. ConocoPhillips, the $38-billion-a-year giant, is drilling for oil in the basement rock of the Black Lion Field off the coast of Vietnam. The company says the field is "unique," and the project is economically feasible because the oil is found at relatively shallow levels in the basement rock. "If you drill deeper into basement rock, you're probably going to find some hydrocarbons, but the chance of finding giant fields is pretty small," says Roger Pinkerton, ConocoPhillips's recently retired head of global exploration. He argues that there are much more accessible—albeit environmentally controversial—sources that will yield plenty of oil for the foreseeable future: to name two, the East Coast of the U.S. and Alaska's National Wildlife Refuge.

Drilling deep into granite probably will never make economic sense unless the industrialized world runs dangerously low on oil or is cut off from its supply. But in the meantime scientists like Thomas Gold, a retired Cornell astronomy professor, are content with poking holes in traditional theories surrounding fossil fuels. It isn't just that hydrocarbons are being discovered in anomalous places like basement rock; Gold notes that primitive hydrocarbons like methane are also found in the atmospheres of Jupiter, Saturn, and other planets.

## One Scientist's Theories

He laid out his theories, which he believes better address those inconsistencies, in his 1998 book, *The Deep Hot Biosphere: The Myth of Fossil Fuels*. He argues that natural gas and oil were created with the earth's formation and reside deep inside the planet. Intense heat and pressure push them from there toward the surface. As to why biological matter (what some deem fossils) is found in oil, Gold says hydrocarbons attract a primitive type of microbe called archaea that lives deep underground; it feeds on and contaminates the oil.

Controversial yet renowned, Gold is credited with figuring out in the 1960s that pulsars were actually radio emissions from rapidly spinning collapsed stars, or neutron stars. To test his non-fossil-fuel theory, Gold in the 1980s persuaded the Swedish government to drill deep in a region near Siljan Lake, about 150 miles north of Stockholm. The Swedes drilled about four miles into basement rock and produced some 80 barrels of oil before the equipment became hopelessly gummed up with putty-like iron oxide. To Gold and his supporters, those 80 barrels were wet, black evidence that oil is no fossil fuel. Critics countered that the oil was merely regurgitated fluid and contaminants from the drilling operation. Because of equipment failures and ballooning costs, the project was abandoned.

Gold insists that the Siljan Lake results have led Soviet scientists and explorers to drill more than 300 deep wells into basement rock since then, producing some oil—but not vast amounts. (In fact, Russian scientists have entertained theories similar to Gold's for as long as 100 years.) "The U.S. petroleum geological community has a viewpoint

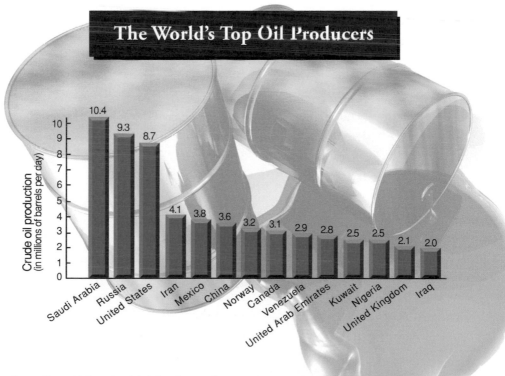

Source: Energy Information Administration, 2004.

firmly opposed to the notion of oil being of nonbiological origin—but not the Russian, Chinese, or Vietnamese," says Gold. "The U.S. has ignored completely the obviously very important Swedish results."

## Additional Oil Theories

Gold isn't the only Western researcher to offer an alternative theory of where oil comes from. Other scientists argue that seismic activity on the ocean floor triggers a geochemical reaction between carbon and hydrogen that produces oil and natural gas. Still others say that bacteria deep within the earth—not dead dinosaurs—are making more oil every day. Scientists from around the world will gather in London [in June 2003] to debate the origins of oil at a conference sponsored by the American Association of Petroleum Geologists and Britain's Institute of Petroleum.

At this point most scientists believe there's a perfectly logical explanation for why fossil fuels can be found in basement rock. "These are fractured rocks where the basement rock has been uplifted and the adjacent sedimentary rocks [that hold decaying plants and animals] pushed into that space," says USGS research geologist Gregory Ulmishek. He adds, "Geology is an empirical science, and we are sure that all the oil and gas that has been found in 150 years of exploration is of a biological nature." Of course, even long-standing scientific doctrines have been proved wrong. There was that little dogma about the earth's being flat.

**EVALUATING THE AUTHORS' ARGUMENTS:**

**In this viewpoint Julie Creswell suggests that the world is not facing an oil crisis. The author of the previous viewpoint, James Howard Kunstler, disagrees. After reading both viewpoints, which author do you agree with? Why?**

# The United States Needs to Pursue Alternative Energy

**Paul Roberts**

*"Not only must we push alternatives such as solar or wind, but new technologies as well."*

In the following viewpoint Paul Roberts criticizes the United States for failing to pursue alternative energy. He urges the U.S. government to support research into solar energy, wind energy, and new energy technology. According to Roberts, efforts by Germany and Japan show how using solar and wind energy can reduce the environmental, economic, and political problems caused by oil. He encourages the United States to become a leader in alternative energy technologies.

Roberts is a journalist who specializes in energy-related issues. He is the author of *The End of Oil: On the Edge of a Perilous New World.*

**AS YOU READ, CONSIDER THE FOLLOWING QUESTIONS:**

1. Why does the author find Ford's use of Japanese hybrid technology "depressing"?

For anyone trying to imagine where America will be getting its energy in two decades, news that Ford's new line of hybrid vehicles will feature a key component of Toyota's hybrid technology was depressing.

Not that Japanese automotive technology is anything to sniff at. When it comes to making gas-electric hybrids that actually sell, Toyota and Honda are the market leaders—meaning Ford will probably have its hybrid on the market much faster than if it developed a complete hybrid system in-house. But that's the rub.

## The United States Is Not Being Aggressive

By outsourcing some of its technology needs to Toyota, Ford has demonstrated yet again how the United States, ostensibly the most technologically advanced nation in history, is losing a key opportunity not only to shape the next energy economy, but perhaps to effectively compete in that economy as well. And given the troubled state of our oil-based energy system, with its growing political, environmental and supply issues, the failure to be an aggressive player in the new energy economy could pose serious long-term problems—especially for countries as energy-hungry as the United States.

**FAST FACT**

The world's biggest solar power plant is in Mulhausen, Germany. It can produce up to 6.3 megawatts of power.

It hasn't always been this way. For nearly a century, U.S. innovations dominated not just the energy business but related businesses, especially automobiles.

Back several decades, when the Arab embargo and the price spikes of the 1970s made the oil economy appear obsolescent, Americans dominated the search for alternatives, such as solar and wind power, in the hopes of cutting U.S. oil imports.

## A Potential Revolution

Government agencies lavished funding on research into solar technologies. Congress granted tax breaks to citizens and companies that bought solar equipment, and it required utilities to buy any excess electricity generated by solar systems or wind farms. America seemed on the verge of an energy revolution. Industry too was on board. Exxon, Arco and Mobil invested heavily in solar technology—not to put it out of business, as some conspiracy theorists believe, or because they thought that solar was intrinsically better than oil, but simply for insurance: If solar did become cost-competitive, Big Oil hoped to control that market as well.

By the mid-1980s, however, the U.S. solar boom had gone bust. Oil prices had fallen dramatically, removing a key incentive for non-oil technologies. Costs for alternatives, such as solar, were still too high to compete with traditional energy sources, such as oil or coal. But the deeper problem was simply that government support had vanished. Even as the Reagan administration moved aggressively to rejuvenate American oil,

*Following the lead of Japanese automakers, the U.S. car industry is developing full-hybrid vehicles, such as this sports utility vehicle manufactured by Ford.*

gas and coal production, providing tax breaks and subsidies worth billions of dollars, the White House was openly hostile to alternative energy. The administration cut R&D funding, and in a grand, symbolic gesture ripped out the solar panels that had been installed on the White House roof by Reagan's Democratic predecessor, Jimmy Carter.

## Germany and Japan Lead the Way

Yet even as America rediscovered fossil fuels, quite another strategy was unfolding elsewhere: Both Germany and Japan began aggressively pushing research in solar, wind and other alternatives. Just as important, both countries have moved to build new markets for alternative technologies—for instance, by subsidizing homeowner purchases of solar panels or helping farmers who want to install wind turbines. By creating more demand, these programs have increased the number of solar cells or wind turbines being manufactured, which is driving down the unit costs—ideally, to the point where alternatives can compete directly with conventional energy.

The results are encouraging. Joachim Luther, director of Germany's Fraunhofer Institute for Solar Energy Systems, a leading solar research center in the world, is upbeat. He says that if current trends in research continue, by as early as 2006 solar energy could be competing, without government subsidies, against coal or gas in sunny regions, such as the Mediterranean, the Middle East and the American Southwest. To be sure, solar will never replace fossil fuels outright. Solar panels take up a lot of space, and their manufacture has its own environmental downsides. Yet solar is growing fast—at 21% a year, or about as fast as cellphones in their early years—and with continued government support and targeted research, this technology could make up a significant portion of the energy mix in the future, thus helping to reduce some of the environmental, political and economic liabilities of our current fossil fuel–dominated system.

So where is the U.S. in all this? On the sidelines. Not only have Germany and Japan far outstripped the United States in solar power ([in 2003,] Japan installed nearly five times as much new solar capacity as America did), but the leading manufacturers of solar technology are companies such as Sharp, Kyocera and Sanyo. In short, even as the solar market appears ready to take off—and provide not just cleaner energy but a new source of jobs and tax revenues—the United States is, relatively speaking, nowhere to be seen.

*Wind turbines, such as these two in southwestern Germany, serve as a major source of energy in Europe.*

Keefe. © 2001 by *Denver Post.* Reproduced by permission of Cagle Cartoons, Inc.

## A Lack of Political Commitment

What's behind America's sluggishness? Certainly, it's not a lack of know-how. At facilities such as the U.S. Energy Department's National Renewable Energy Laboratory in Golden, Colo., for instance, researchers push the limits on solar technology. But what's missing is a political commitment from Washington to give alternatives the same priority as oil, gas and coal.

Not only must we push alternatives such as solar or wind, but new technologies as well. For if the history of technology has taught us anything, it's that solutions don't always come from an expected quarter or in a familiar form. And in the energy economy of the future—which will not only have to supply more energy to more people but do so with fewer resources and fewer emissions—more innovation, not less, is what we'll need.

Sadly, such a push isn't likely under the current administration. President Bush's national energy strategy has promoted traditional energy production even more aggressively than Reagan's did, and has been even more dismissive of alternatives and conservation. At an international conference on development in 2002, the United States joined with such oil-producing countries as Saudi Arabia to defeat a resolution that would have committed all nations to boost renewable energy's share of the global market to 15% by 2010. U.S. officials insisted, with some justification, that such a goal was unrealistic.

But it's also true that many U.S. energy companies (some happened to be major contributors to the president's election campaign) had no interest in a U.S. policy that supported anything but traditional energy systems.

## Wind Energy Struggles

Sadly, such an attitude at the top not only makes it hard to expand America's presence in alternative energy, it actually erodes what small success we've achieved. The American wind industry, for instance, was until recently growing at 30% a year. Helped by a small federal subsidy, U.S. wind farms were nearly cost-competitive with coal-fired power and even cheaper than power plants burning natural gas.

Granted, U.S. wind farms were forced to use turbines imported from Europe, where the wind business is a major source of high-wage jobs that could easily be American. Nonetheless, the fact remained that a form of alternative energy was finally gaining a presence in the U.S. energy market. Unfortunately, Congress [in fall 2003] failed to renew the small government subsidy for wind power. U.S. lawmakers have promised to push for the subsidy later this year, but without a clear signal from the White House, the fate of the program is not clear.

In the meantime, many planned U.S. wind projects are on hold. Experts expect relatively little development in the U.S. wind market this year—even as European wind farmers and European wind-turbine makers brace for another banner year. When it comes to Americans and alternative energy, success, not failure, seems to be our biggest fear.

### EVALUATING THE AUTHOR'S ARGUMENTS:

Paul Roberts discusses how Americans used to be leaders in developing new technologies. After reading his article, consider how America might return to its former position of leadership. What kinds of programs would you suggest starting in order to make that happen?

# Americans Should Become More Energy Efficient

## Hunter Lovins

*"The best way to get off oil . . . is to use what we already have."*

In the following viewpoint Hunter Lovins argues that the best way to avoid an energy crisis is to use traditional sources of energy more efficiently. Lovins explains that innovations such as better-insulated houses and cleaner cars have helped Americans reduce oil consumption and save $200 billion each year. Lovins believes the United States can do even more to improve energy efficiency. For example, he urges American car companies to follow the lead of Japanese and European automakers by making their cars more fuel efficient. Lovins is the coauthor of *Natural Capitalism: Creating the Next Industrial Revolution.*

**AS YOU READ, CONSIDER THE FOLLOWING QUESTIONS:**

1. By what percentage did Americans cut oil consumption between 1979 and 1985, according to the author?
2. According to Lovins, what effect did the imposition of CAFE standards have on fuel efficiency?
3. According to Lovins, how many miles per gallon will the diesel car introduced by Volkswagen get?

For several decades, more efficient use has been the biggest source of new energy—not oil, gas, coal, or nuclear power.

More efficient use of energy enabled Americans after the 1979 oil shock to cut oil consumption 15 percent in six years while the economy grew 16 percent. These efficiencies were achieved by more productive use of energy (better-insulated houses, better-designed lights and electric motors, and cars that are safer, cleaner, more powerful, and get more miles per gallon).

By 2000, the energy service provided by that increased efficiency was 73 percent greater than total U.S. oil consumption, five times domestic oil production, three times all oil imports, and 13 times Persian Gulf oil imports. Since 1996, saved energy has been the nation's fastest-growing major "source" of energy.

In nearly every case, energy efficiency costs far less than the fuel or electricity it saves. It costs only about 2 cents per kilowatt hour to save energy. (Once we've made the easy savings, those costs will go up. However, up to half the energy now used could be saved for that price.) Almost no form of new supply, and few historic ones, can compete with this.

*Americans can make their homes more energy efficient by weather stripping windows, a process that decreases heat loss and lowers energy costs.*

The 40 percent drop in U.S. energy intensity (energy consumption per dollar of real GDP [gross domestic product]) since 1975 has barely dented the potential. The U.S. annual energy bill is about $200 billion lower today than it would have been had we not improved energy efficiency. Yet we are still wasting at least $300 billion a year, and the potential savings keep rising as smarter technologies promise more and better service from less energy. What's even better is that while the side effects of increasing supply are almost uniformly harmful, the side effects of efficiency are beneficial. For example, studies show labor productivity is 6 to 16 percent higher in energy-efficient buildings. . . .

*Hybrid buses, such as this shuttle transporting children to Yosemite National Park, use less gas than traditional buses and offer greater fuel efficiency.*

## Using Energy Efficiently Is Best

Avoiding this cycle of boom-and-bust requires understanding its three root causes:

- Efficiency costs far less than energy supply, so given the choice, most people "buy" it instead.
- Policies that promote both efficiency and supply risk getting both—customers will typically use only one (usually the cheaper one), idling the other.
- Efficiency measures are faster to implement than new supply. Ordinary people are able to implement efficiency long before big, slow, centralized energy generation can be built, let alone paid for.

## Use What We Already Have

The best way to get off oil and implement an energy policy that will give us abundant affordable supplies of energy is to use what we already have dramatically more productively.

The last time this approach was tried, the imposition of CAFE (Corporate Average Fuel Efficiency) standards for vehicles enabled the country to reduce oil purchasing faster and on a larger scale than OPEC [Organization of Petroleum Exporting Countries] could adjust to. New U.S.-built cars increased efficiency seven miles per gallon in six years. Europe achieved similar savings through higher fuel taxes. Together these changes tipped the world oil market in buyers' favor. Between 1977 and 1985, U.S. oil imports fell 42 percent, depriving OPEC of one-eighth of its market. The entire world oil market shrank by one-tenth; OPEC's share was cut from 52 percent to 30 percent, driving down world oil prices. The U.S. alone accounted for one-fourth of that reduction.

Between 1979 and 1986, Americans cut total energy use 5 percent—an intensity drop that was five times greater than the expanded coal and nuclear output subsequently promoted by President Reagan's policy. . . .

## Automobile Efficiency

In 2001, the U.S. National Academy of Sciences reported that cost-effective efficiency efforts could roughly double U.S. fleet efficiency without compromising safety or performance.

*Hybrid cars like the Toyota Prius are becoming more popular as the price of gas continues to rise.*

It is tempting to say that the recent run-up in prices will finally drive even fans of SUVs to rethink their addiction.

It won't.

As the price gets higher—and somewhere over $30 a barrel is enough to get people's attention—substitution begins to occur. With the lessening of demand, price begins to drop. As prices fall, people are all too happy to resume apathy.

Moreover, advertising campaigns (and tax subsidies) that encourage Americans to buy a 10 m.p.g. Hummer2 so that they can paste an American flag on it and feel that they are patriotically supporting the troops, ensure that young men and women will yet again be placed in harm's way, driving 0.5 m.p.g. tanks and 17 feet-per-gallon aircraft carriers.

While American car companies resist making their products more fuel-efficient, the Japanese and Europeans are designing the future. The Toyota Prius hybrid-electric 5-seater gets 48 m.p.g.; Honda's Insight gets 64 m.p.g. If all Americans drove cars that efficient, we would save 32 times the amount of oil that proponents of drilling in the Arctic wilderness hope to find there. Daimler Chrysler and General Motors are testing family sedans at 72 to 80 m.p.g., and Volkswagen sells Europeans a 78-m.p.g. four-seat non-hybrid subcompact.

Almost every automaker at the recent Tokyo Auto Show displayed good hybrid-electric prototypes, some getting 100-plus m.p.g. VW has just premiered an ultra-light but super-safe diesel car that gets 237 miles per gallon.

## Exciting News

There is a lot of progress underway, much of it happening because of concern over climate change, not because of oil prices, but the two go hand-in-hand.

**EVALUATING THE AUTHOR'S ARGUMENTS:**

In this viewpoint Hunter Lovins blames American consumers and advertisers for the popularity of fuel-inefficient sport utility vehicles (SUVs). Why do you think these vehicles are popular? Do you agree with Lovins's view on SUVs? Explain your answers.

# Chapter 2

# Are Alternative Energy Sources Viable?

*Solar panels and wind turbines are two common sources of alternative energy.*

# Nuclear Power Use Should Be Increased

*"[Nuclear power plants] produce large volumes of low-cost electricity around the clock at extremely high levels of safety."*

### Skip Bowman

In the following viewpoint Skip Bowman argues that the United States needs to build more nuclear power plants. According to Bowman, nuclear energy is reliable, afford-able, and clean, which makes it superior to other sources of electricity. He also believes that nuclear waste can be managed safely, thus reducing any danger to the public.

Skip Bowman is the president and chief executive officer of the Nuclear Energy Institute, a policy organization of the nuclear energy industry.

**AS YOU READ, CONSIDER THE FOLLOWING QUESTIONS:**

1. When does Bowman expect companies to break ground on new nuclear plants?
2. According to the author, how many tons of sulfur dioxide was prevented by U.S. reactors?
3. According to Bowman, how much money was spent to investigate the safety of the Yucca Mountain site?

I feel strongly that our national security is tied inextricably to our energy security. . . .

In electricity generation, America clearly faces a growing need for new baseload generating capacity able to meet 24/7 electricity demand. The Energy Department predicts a 45 to 50 percent increase in electricity demand between now and 2025. And we rightly want this new demand to be met by environmentally-friendly generation capacity. Since 1992, when the United States last enacted major energy policy legislation, the industry has built approximately 270,000 megawatts of new gas-fired electric generating capacity. By contrast only 14,000 megawatts of new nuclear and coal-fired capacity have entered service.

Coal and nuclear energy together represent approximately 70 percent of U.S. electricity supply. They provide the highest degree of price stability, but investment in new nuclear and coal-fired power plants has virtually disappeared in the last 10 to 15 years. . . .

*The Diablo Canyon nuclear facility near San Luis Obispo, California, is one of more than one hundred nuclear plants in the United States.*

*A technician at a nuclear power plant in Brazil is dwarfed by two of the facility's massive turbines.*

## Nuclear Plants Are Reliable and Economic

We expect companies to break ground on new nuclear plants in the United States around 2010, with commercial operations beginning as early as 2014. Once those first plants are built and operating, and as companies and investors gain confidence in the new federal licensing process, we expect construction of significant numbers of new reactors after 2015.

Of course, none of this would be possible or plausible unless the industry had a strong foundation on which to build. We have, over the last decade, built that foundation of safe, reliable and economic performance.

The 103 nuclear plants that produce 20 percent of U.S. electricity—about the same percentage, by the way, as here in California—are performing at world-class levels of safety, reliability and efficiency. America's nuclear reactors are operating at capacity factors around 90 percent, and the top nuclear plants (those in the first quartile) are operating at just above 95 percent.

This sustained excellence has increased electricity production from nuclear power plants over the last decade by the equivalent of 18 1,000-megawatt power plants.

## Nuclear Energy Reduces Pollution

U.S. nuclear plants—indeed, nuclear plants around the world—have an obvious value in meeting clean-air requirements and reducing emissions of greenhouse gases. To the extent we build emission-free generating capacity like new nuclear power plants to meet growing electricity demand, we reduce the clean-air compliance burden and costs that would otherwise fall on other types of generating capacity that do produce emissions. We create room underneath emissions caps for the industrial sector and for transportation, and to allow continued economic growth.

In 2004, the 103 U.S. reactors prevented 697 million metric tons of carbon dioxide, and 3.4 million tons of sulfur dioxide and 1.1 million tons of nitrogen oxides—the two pollutants that contribute most to acid rain and smog.

Those are large numbers, and it's tough to relate them to day-to-day experience. Let me put it this way: Without nuclear power, carbon emissions from the U.S. electric sector would be about 30 percent higher. If we shut down all U.S. nuclear plants for a day and wanted to hold carbon emissions constant, the vast majority of Americans would have to park their cars for that day. . . .

## Nuclear Waste Management Has Improved

I want to address one other issue—the elephant in the room, if you will: Management of used nuclear fuel.

Twenty-eight years ago, California imposed a moratorium on new nuclear plant construction unless and until the United States has policies and technologies in place to manage the used nuclear fuel rods. A lot has changed since then—in this area and many others.

In 1977, we did not have the Nuclear Waste Policy Act of 1982.

We did not have the 1987 amendments to the Nuclear Waste Policy Act, which designated the Yucca Mountain site in Nevada as the single site to undergo comprehensive scientific investigation.

We did not have 20 years and $6 billion of scientific investigation that demonstrated that the site is suitable for long-term isolation and management of used nuclear fuel.

We did not have a presidential finding, and affirmation by both houses of Congress, that the Yucca Mountain site is suitable and that the Department of Energy should develop the application necessary to obtain a Nuclear Regulatory Commission license to build and operate the facility.

So, a lot has changed, and it may be appropriate for California to reconsider its policy on this issue. At the very least, an unemotional analysis of the facts is called for. . . .

I believe that we *will* develop technologies to process the waste by-products well beyond mere separation of the valuable uranium and plutonium from the rest of the waste, reducing a 10,000-year disposal challenge to something much shorter and more manageable.

*Yucca Mountain, pictured here, is a proposed site for radioactive waste disposal.*

## The Three Benefits of Nuclear Power

In closing, let me offer a perspective on the strategic value of nuclear energy, and the moral imperatives associated with energy supply.

Nuclear power plants have three distinguishing characteristics. First, they produce large volumes of low-cost electricity around the clock at extremely high levels of safety and reliability. Second, they produce electricity at a stable price, without the punishing volatility we see with gas-fired generating capacity. Third, nuclear plants help maintain our air quality.

Three attributes: Reliable, affordable electricity at low cost. Forward price stability. Clean air.

Other sources of electricity have one or two of these attributes, but only nuclear plants have all three. That is what makes nuclear energy a unique value proposition, and that is why America needs more nuclear energy now.

## EVALUATING THE AUTHOR'S ARGUMENTS:

**Skip Bowman is the president of an organization that represents the nuclear energy industry. Does knowing his background influence the way you interpret his views? If so, in what way?**

# Nuclear Power Use Should Be Eliminated

**Paul and Linda Gunter**

*"A terrorist attack on just a single U.S. nuclear plant could deliver the unimaginable."*

Nuclear power is unsafe and should not be pursued by the United States, Paul and Linda Gunter argue in the following viewpoint. They discuss the 1986 accident at the Chernobyl atomic reactor in the Ukraine to show that a similar meltdown at an American plant could make millions of people very sick. They also argue that a terrorist attack on a nuclear plant could lead to thousands of deaths. For these reasons, they urge Americans to avoid using nuclear power.

Paul and Linda Gunter are the director of the Reactor Watchdog Project and the director of media relations, respectively, at the Nuclear Information and Resource Service. NIRS provides information about issues surrounding nuclear power.

**AS YOU READ, CONSIDER THE FOLLOWING QUESTIONS:**
1. How many nuclear reactors were operating in the United States as of May 2005, according to the authors?
2. As stated by the Gunters, what radiation-linked diseases have affected Ukrainians?
3. According to a study cited by the authors, how many people could die from cancer if terrorists struck a nuclear plant near Manhattan?

Paul and Linda Gunter, "Chernobyl Can Happen Here," *Liberal Opinion Week,* June 8, 2005, p. 24. Reproduced by permission of the authors.

T he 19th anniversary of the Chernobyl atomic reactor disaster in Ukraine slipped by [in April 2005] with scarcely a murmur in the media.

Instead, headlines were trumpeting the new nuclear "renaissance," as the Bush administration flaunts its pork-laden energy bill and the industry crows about "clean, green, nuclear power."

## Ignoring the Horrors

In attempting to muscle its way into the climate change argument, with a barrage of misinformation and flawed statistics, the nuclear industry is conveniently ducking the very real horrors that would ensue if one of their reactors suffered an accident or attack resulting in a release to the environment of its radioactive contents. And the weight of scientific evidence suggests such an outcome is not only possible but also probable.

Since [the terrorist attacks of] 9/11, the security landscape has changed forever. We know that an attack on a U.S. reactor was in the original al Qaeda plans and likely will be again. The 103 operating U.S. reactors are all now reaching the end of their life spans, meaning they are more prone to technical problems that could lead to accident. And despite their geriatric status, older reactors are subject to fewer safety checks and are run hotter and longer, leading to cracking and embrittled parts vulnerable to failure.

The U.S. Nuclear Regulatory Commission (NRC), congressionally charged with safeguarding the public, has instead capitulated to the industry's profit-margin priorities. Added to that, older reactors contain radiation inventories far larger than the infant reactor at Chernobyl that had operated for just two years before the catastrophe. And of course, both the Chernobyl and Three Mile Island[1] accidents were a

> **FAST FACT**
>
> Nuclear waste is so toxic that the Environmental Protection Agency requires it be kept physically separate from the environment for ten thousand years.

---

1. A nuclear power plant in Pennsylvania experienced a partial core meltdown in March 1979.

result of human error, the one wild card that can never be entirely eliminated.

## The Health Consequences of Chernobyl

Also forgotten amidst the Washington pundits' pro-nuclear pronouncements are the tragic consequences so vividly seen today in the children of Chernobyl. These are young lives forever altered by the birth defects they inherited from their parents who had the misfortune to live close to the reactor or downwind of its toxic fallout cloud. Many have been abandoned in orphanages. More than seven million people in the former Soviet Republics of Belarus, Russia and Ukraine are believed to have suffered medical problems and genetic damage as the

*This young boy from Belarus suffers from leukemia caused by radiation from the 1986 meltdown of the Chernobyl nuclear power plant.*

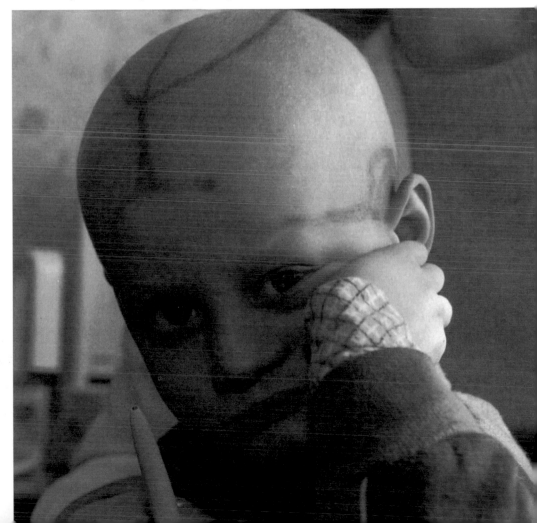

direct result of Chernobyl. In Ukraine alone, more than 2.3 million people, including 452,000 children, have been treated for radiation-linked illnesses, including thyroid and blood cancers and cancerous growths, according to the Ukrainian Ministry of Health.

New findings reported last November [2004] in the "Journal of Epidemiology and Community Health" published by the British Medical Association concluded that more than 800 cancers in Sweden are being attributed to the ever-widening impact of the "Chernobyl effect."

## A Potential Catastrophe

It is increasingly disingenuous of the nuclear industry to distance itself from a potential catastrophic accident in the United States.

*The possibility of terrorist attacks on Three Mile Island (pictured) and other U.S. nuclear facilities has prompted increased security measures.*

Kirk. © 2002 by Kirk Anderson. Reproduced by permission.

Considerable evidence exists that currently operating U.S. reactor containments can also fail during a severe accident. A 1990 U.S. Nuclear Regulatory Commission (NRC) study of risks associated with severe reactor accidents concluded that none of the five different U.S. designs it analyzed were capable of remaining intact during all severe accident scenarios.

Furthermore, a terrorist attack on just a single U.S. nuclear plant could deliver the unimaginable. One study that examined such a catastrophe at the Indian Point nuclear plant just 25 miles from Manhattan, concluded that the number of near-term deaths within 50 miles, due to lethal radiation exposures received within seven days after an attack by a large aircraft would number approximately 44,000 under worst case scenario weather conditions. Long-term cancer deaths could soar as high as 500,000. Manhattan would become a near-permanent sacrifice zone.

## America's Choice

The recently released National Academy of Sciences report on the vulnerability of reactor fuel pools supports these conclusions.

According to the report, an attack on a fuel pool and the resulting fire "would create thermal plumes that could potentially transport radioactive aerosols hundreds of miles downwind under appropriate atmospheric conditions."

Fortunately, Americans have a choice. We can reject the nuclear liability and tell our elected representatives to advocate for energy efficiency and renewable energy, measures that carry none of the dangers nor the toxic legacy of nuclear power. It's common sense. And our children's children will thank us.

## EVALUATING THE AUTHORS' ARGUMENTS:

The authors of this viewpoint and the previous viewpoint disagree over whether nuclear power plants are safe. Which author(s) do you believe made the more convincing argument? Was there a particular piece of evidence that swayed you? Explain.

# Wind Energy Should Be Pursued

## Bill McKibben

*"Wind power is . . . the fastest-growing source of electric generation."*

In the following viewpoint Bill McKibben argues that the United States needs to expand its use of wind power. According to McKibben, using more wind power can help solve the problem of global warming. He also writes that while wind farms may mar the picturesque landscape of the American wilderness, their environmental benefits outweigh any visual drawbacks.

McKibben is a leading environmentalist. His works include *The End of Nature*.

**AS YOU READ, CONSIDER THE FOLLOWING QUESTIONS:**
1. As explained by the author, why is wind power being used more than solar power?
2. According to McKibben, what did a University of New Hampshire computer simulation reveal about global warming?
3. How does the author say his love of nature has influenced his opinion of wind power?

Bill McKibben, "Tilting at Windmills: When the Price Is Worth Paying," *The New York Times,* February 16, 2005. Copyright © 2005 by the New York Times Company. Reproduced by permission.

Finally, American environmentalists have a chance to get it right about wind power.

News broke [in February 2005] of plans for the first big wind energy installation in Adirondack Park. Ten towering turbines would sprout on the site of an old garnet mine in this tiny town. They'd be visible from the ski slopes at nearby Gore Mountain, and they'd be visible too from the deep wild of the Siamese Ponds Wilderness, one of the loneliest and most beautiful parts of New York's "forever wild" Adirondack Forest Preserve, the model for a century of American conservation. In fact, it would be hard to imagine a place better suited to illustrate the controversy that wind power is causing in this country.

I know the area well; I've lived most of my adult life in this part of the world, and I've skied and backpacked through the old mine and the woods around it, searched for (and found) lost hunters, encountered its bears and coyotes and fishers, sat on its anonymous peaks and

*Two people watch as a crane lifts into place the blades of a giant wind turbine in eastern England.*

*Wind energy is the fastest-growing source of energy in the world. This enormous turbine in Germany is the largest on Earth.*

knolls and watched the hawks circle beneath. In fact, this very wilderness—these yellow birches, the bear that left that berry-filled pile of scat, those particular loons laughing on that particular lake—led me to fall in love with the world outdoors. Which is precisely why I hope those wind turbines rise on the skyline, and as soon as possible.

## Wind Power's Slow Rise in America

The planet faces many environmental challenges, but none of them come close to global warming. In [February 2005] new studies have shown that the trigger point for severe climate change may be closer than previously thought, and the possible consequences even more severe. Just to slow the pace of this rapid warming will require every possible response, from more efficient cars to fewer sprawling suburbs to more trains to—well, the list is pretty well endless. But wind power is one key component.

*Erected in late 2005, these windmills provide the first source of alternative energy in the Philippines.*

Around the world it's the fastest-growing source of electric generation, mostly because the technology, unlike solar power, has evolved to the point where it's cost-competitive with fossil fuels. The Danes already generate nearly a quarter of their power from the breeze; the Germans and the Spaniards and the British are rapidly heading in the same direction.

In America, however, the growth of wind power has been slower. Partly that's because the Bush administration's stance on climate change has meant scant government support for renewable energy. But partly, too, it's because environmentalists, particularly in the crowded East, haven't come to terms with this technology. In fights in Cape Cod, the mountains of Vermont, and the ridgelines of Maryland, they've divided into bitter factions over almost every turbine proposal. On one side, national environmental groups like Greenpeace have backed many installations, arguing that the dangers of global warming far outweigh any local effects. On the other side, neighbors of proposed wind farms have joined with local chapters of big conservation groups to fight the Statue-of-Liberty-size windmills on environmental grounds, chiefly arguing that they'll destroy the scenic beauty of their areas.

That may be provincial, but it's not entirely inaccurate. These newer, more efficient turbines are enormous; part of me doesn't want to gaze out from the summit of Peaked Mountain or the marsh at Thirteenth Lake and see an industrial project in the distance. In the best of all possible worlds, we'd do without them.

## Wind or Warming

But it's not the best of all possible worlds. Right now, the choice is between burning fossil fuels and making the transition, as quickly as possible, to renewable power. There are more than 100 coal-fired power plants on the drawing board in this country right now; if they are built we will spew ever more carbon into the atmosphere. And that will endanger not only the residents of low-lying tropical nations that will be swamped by rising oceans, but also the residents of the Siamese Pond Wilderness. The birch and beech and maple that turn this place glorious in the fall won't survive a rapid warming; the computer modeling for this part of the country, conducted at the University of New Hampshire, shows that if we continue with business as usual there won't even be winter as we've known it here by century's end, just one long chilly mud season. . . .

So here environmentalists should step back and say, especially in this cradle of American wilderness, that the price is worth paying. To see that blade turning in the blue Adirondack sky—to see the breeze made visible—should be a sign of real hope for the future.

**EVALUATING THE AUTHOR'S ARGUMENTS:**

In this viewpoint, Bill McKibben supports the use of wind power, but explains why many environmentalists are critical of windmills. If you agree with McKibben, how would you convince those who oppose him? Or, do you believe the critics of wind power have a valid argument? Explain your answers.

# Viewpoint 4

# Wind Energy Has Many Drawbacks

## H. Sterling Burnett

"*Wind power's . . . significant environmental harms are often ignored.*"

Wind power is bad for the environment and cannot replace fossil fuels, H. Sterling Burnett claims in the following viewpoint. He argues that wind farms do not reduce air pollution and are deadly to migratory birds and bats. Wind farms, in the author's opinion, are also noisy and use up significant amounts of land while producing very little energy. Burnett concludes that wind power's many problems make it unsuitable for government funding.

Burnett is a senior fellow with the National Center for Policy Analysis, a public policy research organization.

**AS YOU READ, CONSIDER THE FOLLOWING QUESTIONS:**

1. In the author's opinion what is the main reason wind power does not reduce air pollution?
2. According to Burnett, how much power would a proposed twenty-four-square-mile wind farm in Massachusetts produce?
3. In addition to birds, what other species have been killed by wind turbines, as listed by Burnett?

H. Sterling Burnett, "Wind Power Puffery," *The Washington Times,* February 4, 2004. Copyright © 2004 by the Washington Times. All rights reserved. Reproduced by permission of Valeo IP.

W henever there is a discussion of energy policy, many environmentalists and their political allies tout wind power as an alternative to burning fossil fuels. Even if electricity from wind power is more expensive than conventional fuel sources, and it is, wind advocates argue its environmental benefits are worth it. In particular, proponents claim increased reliance on wind power would reduce air pollution and greenhouse gas emissions.

But is this assertion correct? No, the truth is wind power's environmental benefits are usually overstated, while its significant environmental harms are often ignored.

## The Limitations of Wind Farms

Close inspection of wind power finds that promised air pollution improvements do not materialize. There are several reasons, the principal one being that wind farms generate power only when the wind blows within a certain range of speed. When there is too little wind,

*Critics of windmills maintain that wind farms are unsightly, dangerous to migratory birds, and generate insignificant amounts of energy.*

wind towers don't generate power. Conversely, when the wind is too strong, they must be shut off for fear of being blown down.

Due to this fundamental limitation, wind farms need conventional power plants to supplement the power they supply and to replace a wind farm's expected supply to the grid when the towers are not turning. After all, the power grid requires a regulated constant flow of energy to function properly.

Yet bringing a conventional power plant on line to supply power is not as simple as turning on a switch. Most "redundant" fossil fuel power stations must run, even if at reduced levels, continuously. When

*The proposed placement of wind turbines near England's Lake District has generated intense debate. The turbine pictured here is six miles from the proposed site.*

these factors are combined with the emissions of pollutants and $CO_2$ caused by the manufacture and maintenance of wind towers and their associated infrastructure, very little of the air quality improvements actually result from expansion of wind power.

## Noisy and Ugly

There are other problems. A recent report from Great Britain—where wind power is growing even faster than in the U.S.—says that as wind farms grow, wind power is increasingly unpopular. Why? Wind farms are noisy, land-intensive and unsightly. The industry has tricked its way into unspoiled countryside in "green" disguise by portraying wind farms as "parks." In reality, wind farms are more similar to highways, industrial buildings, railways and industrial farms. This wouldn't be a major consideration if it weren't that, because of the prevailing wind currents, the most favorable locations for wind farms usually are areas with particularly spectacular views in relatively wild places.

Worse, wind farms produce only a fraction of the energy of a conventional power plant but require hundreds of times the acreage. For instance, two of the biggest wind "farms" in Europe have 159 turbines and cover thousands of acres between them. But together they take a year to produce less than four days' output from a single 2,000-megawatt conventional power station—which takes up 100 times fewer acres. And in the U.S., a proposed wind farm off the coast of Massachusetts would produce only 450 megawatts of power but require 130 towers and more than 24 square miles of ocean.

## A Danger to Animals

Perhaps the most well-publicized harmful environmental impact of wind power relates to its effect on birds and bats. For efficiency, wind farms must be located where the wind blows fairly constantly.

Scherer. © 2005 by Randy Scherer. Reproduced by permission.

Unfortunately, such locations are prime travel routes for migratory birds, including protected species like bald and golden eagles. This motivated the Sierra Club to label wind towers "the Cuisinarts of the air."

Indeed, scientists estimate as many as 44,000 birds have been killed over the past 20 years by wind turbines in the Altamont Pass, east of San Francisco. The victims include kestrels, red-tailed hawks and golden eagles—an average of 50 golden eagles are killed each year.

These problems are exacerbated explains one study as "Wind farms have been documented to act as both bait and executioner—rodents taking shelter at the base of turbines multiply with the protection from raptors, while in turn their greater numbers attract more raptors to the farm."

Deaths are not limited to the United States or to birds. For example, at Tarif, Spain, thousands of birds from more than 13 species protected under European Union law have been killed by the site's 269 wind turbines. During [fall 2003's] migration, at least 400 bats, including red bats, eastern pipistrelles, hoary bats and possible endangered Indiana bats, were killed at a 44-turbine wind farm in West Virginia.

## Wind Power Is No Bargain

As a result of these problems and others, lawsuits are either pending or being considered to prevent expansion of wind farms in West Virginia and California and to prevent the construction of offshore wind farms in a number of New England states.

Indeed, the Audubon Society has called for a moratorium on new wind development in bird-sensitive areas—which, because of the climatic conditions needed for wind farms, includes the vast majority of the suitable sites for proposed construction.

Wind power is expensive, doesn't deliver the environmental benefits it promises and has substantial environmental costs. In short, wind power is no bargain. Accordingly, it doesn't merit continued government promotion or funding.

### EVALUATING THE AUTHORS' ARGUMENTS:

While authors Bill McKibben and H. Sterling Burnett both agree that wind farms can be unsightly, they disagree on whether that is a serious drawback. Whose view do you find more convincing and why?

## Viewpoint 5

# Solar Power Should Be Pursued

**Amanda Griscom**

*"As the nation cries out for energy independence, going solar is really becoming the ultimate patriotic act."*

In the following viewpoint Amanda Griscom profiles the Hathaways, a family who has built a house powered solely by solar energy. According to Griscom, the attractive appearance, fuel efficiency, and lower energy costs of the Hathaway home show that solar energy can be part of a regular lifestyle. She concludes that as more families follow the Hathaways' lead, America will become energy independent and cause less damage to the environment.

Griscom is an energy analyst for the environmental consulting firm GreenOrder and a columnist for the environmental online magazine *Grist*.

**AS YOU READ, CONSIDER THE FOLLOWING QUESTIONS:**

1. As explained by Griscom, what are three energy-saving technologies used in the Hathaway house?
2. According to the Department of Energy, what is the average annual energy bill for a detached house?
3. Between 1999 and 2003, by what percentage did the cost of solar technology decrease, according to the author?

Amanda Griscom, "The Solar Patriot," *Mother Earth News,* August/September 2003. Copyright © 2003 by Ogden Publications, Inc. All rights reserved. Reproduced by permission.

When Alden Hathaway told his wife, Carol, that he wanted to build a totally self-sufficient, solar-powered home for their family of five, she feared that it was the end of life as she knew it: She wasn't ready to give up her clothes dryer and dishwasher to conserve energy, along with her morning ritual of curling her hair. . . .

In the end, he built his solar dream home and she got to keep her dishwasher, clothes dryer and, yes, even the heat rollers for her hair.

*Sherry Boschert, president of the San Francisco Electric Vehicle Association, stands beside her electric vehicle in front of her solar-powered home.*

## High-Tech and Energy-Efficient

Alden's idealism and Carol's pragmatism turned out to be the perfect combination. In the summer of 2001, the couple built a house that satisfied them both: spacious, fully solar-powered, located in a choice neighborhood and replete with plug-in creature comforts—including all the gadgetry coveted by their digital-era children: Tripp, 15; Mary, 13; and Megan, 12. . . .

The result, on a 4.8-acre site in northern Virginia near Purcellville, is a house so commodious, cutting-edge and cost-effective that it's at the vanguard of a much-needed, larger movement: the growth of solar suburbia. . . .

## The Technology Is Practically Invisible

"Most people assume a solar house is a spaceship-looking thing with boxy modules and antennas sticking out of it, or a junky eco-shack in

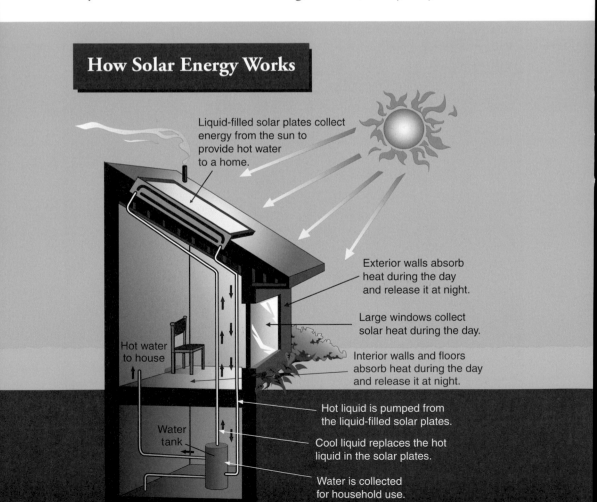

**How Solar Energy Works**

Liquid-filled solar plates collect energy from the sun to provide hot water to a home.

Exterior walls absorb heat during the day and release it at night.

Large windows collect solar heat during the day.

Hot water to house

Interior walls and floors absorb heat during the day and release it at night.

Hot liquid is pumped from the liquid-filled solar plates.

Water tank

Cool liquid replaces the hot liquid in the solar plates.

Water is collected for household use.

the woods," says Alden. "We wanted the design of our home to prove that solar can be attractive to the masses."

They found a nearby property with fewer restrictions and, with careful design decisions, were able to make the technology practically invisible. [Builder Don] Bradley used thin-film photovoltaic (PV) modules from a company called Uni-Solar. The flexible material can be cut, peeled and seamlessly pasted onto a generic metal roof. For maximum solar production,

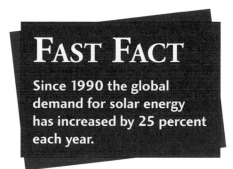

**FAST FACT**

Since 1990 the global demand for solar energy has increased by 25 percent each year.

he positioned the house to face due south, angling the roof to capture the arc of the sun's movement, and created a breezeway between the house and the garage to eliminate any shading of the rooftop panels. . . .

Because Carol and the three young Hathaways aren't exactly abstemious about their electricity use—the house has four computers, three televisions, two Nintendo systems, three stereos and a full complement of domestic appliances—Alden built a hefty 6-kilowatt solar energy system that spans 1,000 square feet on the rooftops of the house and garage.

In addition to the photovoltaic panels, the house uses other renewable technologies: Solar thermal panels heat the water and a geothermal system provides space heating and air conditioning. The latter is a labyrinth of pipes sunk 5 feet underground, where the earth is a constant temperature of 58 degrees. A heat-transfer fluid pumped through the pipe system heats the house in the winter and cools it in the summer.

## Costs and Savings

In August 2001, the Hathaway family moved into their new home. With the Department of Energy [DOE] monitoring daily electricity use, they have completed a successful test run in one of America's first "zero net-energy" homes. A zero net-energy home produces its own power, usually from solar panels, but is connected to the electricity grid used by traditional houses. It draws power from the utility

*This array of solar panels, which is approximately the size of a football field, can provide enough energy for the needs of one thousand homes in Barcelona, Spain.*

whenever necessary—when the sun isn't shining—and pumps its own "green" electricity back into the grid when it produces a surplus. It's a zero-sum game: Nights balance out against days, sunny summer months balance out against dark winter months. Over a full year, a zero net-energy house produces at least as much electricity as it consumes.

Next to car and mortgage payments, energy bills are one of the largest household expenses for most U.S. families today. The average annual energy bill for a detached house is $1,570, according to the DOE. The Hathaway house, in contrast, has an annual energy bill of $300, or $25 a month, which includes the cost of the connect fee.

Of course, the energy-saving technology doesn't come free. But the Hathaways developed a long-term financing plan to manage the added costs. In total, the energy technology cost an additional $45,000 (the house cost $320,000), but increased the monthly mortgage payments by only 10 percent. So far, their savings in energy bills is about $260 a month, which offsets the increased payments. . . .

The Hathaways' economic savings translates into environmental savings, too: Factoring in both their clean-energy system and hybrid gas-electric car, the family has reduced their average annual carbon dioxide emissions by 40 percent. And, best of all, they say, the savings come without concessions in performance and without sacrificing their standard of living. . . .

## The Increasing Popularity of Solar Energy

Though the family's keen energy awareness isn't exactly typical, their shift toward energy independence does reflect a nationwide trend. The demand for solar panels across the country has been increasing at more than 20 percent per year [since 1999] according to the DOE. During that period, the cost of solar technology has plunged nearly 50 percent, thanks to manufacturing innovations that make more mainstream applications possible. . . .

## The Biggest Challenge of Our Time

According to David Garman, assistant secretary of the DOE's Office of Energy Efficiency and Renewable Energy, 18 million new houses will be built in this country between now and 2010. The DOE is researching ways to reduce energy use in those new homes by up to 50 percent; it plans to encourage consumers by establishing special incentives for new energy-efficient homes and appliances, as well as photovoltaic systems and solar water heaters. Garman says data taken from the Hathaways' zero net-energy house is helping to make this goal possible. . . .

"As the nation cries out for energy independence," says Bradley, "going solar is really becoming the ultimate patriotic act."

**EVALUATING THE AUTHOR'S ARGUMENTS:**

Consider the solar-powered house described by Griscom in this viewpoint. Do you think that this kind of house is practical or is it unlikely to replace traditional types of homes? Explain your answer.

# Solar Power Should Not Be Pursued

*"The fossil fuel savings and environmental benefits of solar are considerably smaller than many proponents suggest."*

**Ben Lieberman**

Solar energy has many drawbacks, Ben Lieberman argues in the following viewpoint. He points out that solar energy cannot be continually created—only when the sun is out. Furthermore, the cost of solar energy systems far outweighs the amount of electricity that they create, he argues. Lieberman concludes that while solar energy may be politically correct, it is a poor investment that should not receive government support.

Lieberman is a senior policy analyst at the Heritage Foundation.

**AS YOU READ, CONSIDER THE FOLLOWING QUESTIONS:**
1. According to the author, what is the dollar value of the electricity generated by a $5,000 rooftop photovoltaic system?
2. Why do solar panels need to be replaced, as explained by Lieberman?
3. In what way does the author believe the pro-solar crowd has misled consumers?

The Solar Decathlon is underway, and teams of students from 14 colleges and universities are building solar-powered homes on the National Mall in Washington DC in an effort to promote this alternative energy source. [In September 2002] judges in this Department of Energy (DOE) sponsored event will evaluate these homes and declare one the winner. Unfortunately for the participants, it rained on the Sept 26th opening ceremonies, and the skies over Washington have remained mostly overcast since. However, the conditions may have made for a more revealing demonstration of solar energy than was originally planned.

Although the Solar Decathlon's purpose is to hawk the benefits of electricity-generating solar panels and other residential solar gadgets, the bad weather has made it hard to ignore the limitations. As fate so amply demonstrated, not every day is a sunny day, and indeed DOE's "Solar Village on the National Mall" has received very little of what it needs to run.

*Workers install a solar panel on an Oregon home. Although many people are turning toward solar energy, critics contend that it is expensive and inefficient.*

## Solar Energy Does Not Save Money

Since solar is not a 24/7 energy source, even a community consisting entirely of solar homes and businesses would still need to be connected to a constantly-running power plant (most likely natural gas or coal fired) to provide reliable electricity. For this reason, the fossil fuel savings and environmental benefits of solar are considerably smaller than many proponents suggest.

*Opponents of solar energy note that solar panels are of little use on cloudy days like this one in Salem, Oregon.*

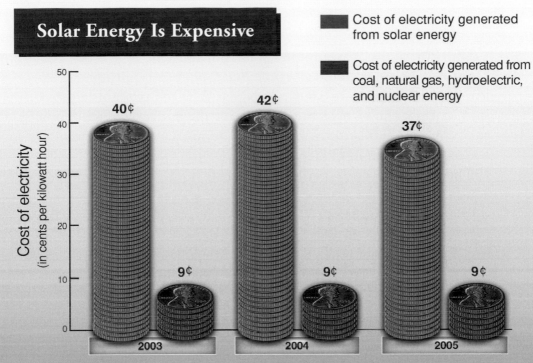

## Solar Energy Is Expensive

**Cost of electricity generated from solar energy**

**Cost of electricity generated from coal, natural gas, hydroelectric, and nuclear energy**

Cost of electricity (in cents per kilowatt hour)

40¢   42¢   37¢
9¢    9¢    9¢

2003   2004   2005

Source: Exxon Mobile, "A Report on Energy Trends, Greenhouse Gas Emissions, and Alternative Energy," February 2004.

Washington DC gets its share of sunny days as well, but even so, solar equipment provides only a modest amount of energy in relation to its cost. In fact, a $5,000 rooftop photovoltaic system typically generates no more than $100 of electricity per year, providing a rate of return comparable to a passbook savings account.

Nor do the costs end when the system is installed. Like anything exposed to the elements, solar equipment is subject to wear and storm damage, and may need ongoing maintenance and repairs. In addition, the materials that turn sunlight into electricity degrade over time. Thus, solar panels will eventually need to be replaced, most likely before the investment has fully paid itself off in the form of reduced utility bills.

## Political Silliness

Few things are as politically-correct as solar energy, and it has always had its share of true believers willing to pay extra to feel good about their homes and themselves. But for homeowners who view it as an investment, it is not a good one. The economic realities are rarely acknowledged by the government officials and solar equipment manufacturers involved in the Solar Decathlon and similarly one-sided promotions. By failing to be objective, the pro-solar crowd does consumers a real disservice.

Unfortunately, Washington's solar silliness extends to the U.S. Capitol. This event comes at a time that Congress is putting the finishing touches on its massive energy bill. The bill contains a provision to revive the 15 percent tax credit for the purchase of residential solar equipment, instituted in 1978 by Jimmy Carter but later killed by Ronald Reagan in 1986.[1]

The previous tax credit encouraged many homeowners to buy solar equipment. Most of them learned the hard way that even subsidized solar is a money pit. But today, there's a whole new generation of gullible homeowners who lack any direct experience with residential solar and may fall for the sales pitch, especially if the tax break is brought back.

Like the participants in the Solar Decathlon, they're going to get soaked.

1. Congress failed to pass an energy bill in 2002.

## EVALUATING THE AUTHORS' ARGUMENTS:

Amanda Griscom and Ben Lieberman reach opposing conclusions about the benefits of solar-powered homes. Whose argument do you find more convincing? Why?

# Chapter 3

# Should Alternatives to Gasoline-Powered Vehicles Be Pursued?

*A large percentage of the world's oil supply goes to providing fuel for automobiles, such as these Volkswagens.*

**Viewpoint 1**

# Hybrid Cars Will Reduce U.S. Oil Dependence

## Lester R. Brown

*"Gas-electric hybrid engines and advanced-design wind turbines offer a way to wean ourselves from imported oil."*

In the following viewpoint Lester R. Brown argues that one way to reduce American reliance on imported oil is by building cars that run on either gas-electric hybrid engines or automobiles that run on wind-generated electricity. Combining the two technologies could be even more beneficial, he argues. According to Brown, creating cars that run on both types of energy will be affordable, will strengthen local economies, will greatly reduce the amount of oil Americans use, and slash carbon emissions.

Brown is the founder and president of the Earth Policy Institute, an organization whose goal is an environmentally sustainable economy.

**AS YOU READ, CONSIDER THE FOLLOWING QUESTIONS:**
1. How many hybrid-powered buses has General Motors sent to Seattle, according to Brown?
2. According to the author, how tall is the average wind turbine?
3. In the author's opinion how can the irregularity of wind energy be offset?

W ith the price of oil above $50 a barrel, political instability in the Middle East on the rise, and little slack in the world oil economy, we need a new energy strategy. Fortunately, a new strategy is emerging using two new technologies.

## Reducing Gasoline Use with Wind and Electricity

Gas-electric hybrid engines and advanced-design wind turbines offer a way to wean ourselves from imported oil. If over the next decade we convert the U.S. automobile fleet to gas-electric hybrids with the efficiency of today's Toyota Prius, we could cut our gasoline use in half. No change in the number of vehicles, no change in miles driven—just doing it more effeciently. Several gas-electric hybrid car models are now on the market including the Toyota Prius, the Honda Insight and the hybrid version of the Honda Civic. The Prius—a midsize car on the cutting-edge of auto technology,—gets an astounding 55 mpg in combined city/highway driving. No wonder lists of eager buyers are willing to wait six months or more for delivery.

*An auto assembler works on a Ford Escape sports utility vehicle, the world's first hybrid SUV.*

Many other hybrid vehicles are beginning to appear in showrooms, or are scheduled to arrive soon. Ford has recently released a hybrid model of its Escape SUM, Honda has released a hybrid version of its popular Accord sedan, and General Motors will offer hybrid versions of several of its cars and trucks, including the Chevy Tahoe, the Chevy Malibu and the Saturn VUE. Beyond this, GM has delivered 235 hybrid-powered buses to Seattle. Other large cities slated to get hybrid buses are Philadelphia, Houston and Portland.

## The Potential for Wind-Generated Electricity

With gas-electric hybrid vehicles now on the market, the stage is set for the second step to reduce oil dependence: the use of wind-generated electricity to power automobiles. If we add to the gas-electric hybrid a plug-in capacity and a second battery [to] increase its electricity storage capacity, motorists could then do their commuting, shopping and other short-distance travel largely with electricity, saving gasoline for the occasional long trip. This could lop another 20 percent off gasoline use in addition to the initial 50-percent cut from shifting to gas-electric hybrids, for a total reduction of 70 percent.

Cole. © by Cagle Cartoons, Inc. Reproduced by permission.

The plug-in capacity gives access to the country's vast, largely untapped wind resources. In 1991, the U.S. Department of Energy published a National Wind Resource Inventory in which it pointed out that three states—Kansas, North Dakota and Texas—have enough harnessable wind energy to satisfy national electricity needs. Many were astonished by this news since wind power was widely considered a marginal energy source. Yet in retrospect, we know this was a gross underestimate simply because it was based on the wind turbine technologies of 1991. Advances in design since then enable turbines to operate at lower wind speeds and to convert wind into electricity more efficiently.

The average turbine in 1991 was roughly 120 feet tall, whereas new ones are 300 feet tall—the height of a 30-story building. Not only does this more than double the amount of harvestable wind, but winds at the higher elevation are stronger and more reliable.

## Wind Power Success Stories

In Europe, which has emerged as the world leader in developing wind energy, wind farms now satisfy the residential electricity needs of 40 million consumers. In 2003, the European Wind Energy Association projected that by 2020 this energy source would provide electricity for 195 million people—half the population of Western Europe. A 2004 assessment of Europe's offshore potential by the Garrad Hassan consulting group concluded that if European governments move vigorously to develop this potential, wind could supply all of the region's residential electricity by 2020. Wind power is growing fast because it is cheap, abundant, inexhaustible, widely distributed, clean and climate-benign. No other energy source has all of these attributes.

The cost of wind-generated electricity has been in free fall over the last two decades. The early wind farms in California, where the modern wind industry was born in the 1980s, generated electricity at a cost of 38 cents per kilowatt-hour. Now many wind farms are producing power at 4 cents per kilowatt-hour, and some long-term supply contracts have

*A helicopter approaches the world's largest wind power station in Germany. In the future, wind power may be used to charge storage batteries in cars.*

recently been signed at 3 cents per kilowatt-hour. And the price is still falling.

## Cost-Effective and Environmentally Friendly

Unlike the widely discussed fuel cell/hydrogen transportation model, the gas-electric hybrid/wind model does not require a costly new infrastructure; the network of gasoline service stations is already in place. So, too, is the electricity grid needed to link wind farms to the storage batteries in cars. For this new model to work most efficiently, we would need a strong integrated national grid. Fortunately, the need for modernizing our antiquated set of regional grids, and replacing them with a strong national grid, is now widely recognized, especially after the 2003 blackout that darkened portions of the northeast United States and southeast Canada.

One of the few weaknesses of wind energy—its irregularity—is largely offset with the use of plug-in gas-electric hybrids, as the batteries in these vehicles become a part of the storage system for wind energy. Beyond this, there is always the tank of gasoline as a backup. . . .

Communities in rural America desperately want to earn the additional revenue from wind farms and the jobs they bring. In addition, money spent on electricity generated from wind farms stays in the community, creating a ripple effect throughout the local economy. Within a matter of years, thousands of farmers could be earning far more from electricity sales than from farming.

Moving to highly efficient gas-electric hybrids with plug in capacity, combined with the construction of thousands of wind farms across the country that feed electricity into a national grid, will give us the energy security that has eluded us for three decades. It also will rejuvenate farm and ranch communities, and shrink the U.S. balance-of-trade deficit. Even more important, it will dramatically cut carbon emissions, making the United States a model that other countries can emulate.

## EVALUATING THE AUTHOR'S ARGUMENTS:

After reading Lester R. Brown's viewpoint, would you consider purchasing or driving a hybrid car? If so, which of his arguments did you find the most convincing? If not, what do you consider the drawbacks of these vehicles? Explain your answers.

# Alternative-Fuel Cars Are Bad for the Environment

**Andrew Kantor**

*"Electric cars are dirty. . . . They might even be more dirty than their gasoline-powered cousins."*

Cars that run on electricity or ethanol (a fuel produced from corn) are bad for the environment, Andrew Kantor argues in the following viewpoint. According to Kantor, the process used to create ethanol releases carbon monoxide and other pollutants into the air. He also argues that electric cars are dirtier than traditional vehicles because coal is burned to create the electricity. Kantor concludes that gasoline-fueled cars are clean and efficient and should not be replaced by alternative-fuel automobiles.

Kantor is the technology columnist for USAToday.com, the Web site of *USA Today*.

**AS YOU READ, CONSIDER THE FOLLOWING QUESTIONS:**
1. What does the word *touted* mean in the context of the viewpoint?
2. How many pounds of corn are needed to make one gallon of ethanol, according to the author?
3. What are the by-products of the ethanol distillation process, as explained by Kantor?

Andrew Kantor, "Green Technology Isn't Always Very Green," www.usatoday.com, June 24, 2005. Copyright © 2005 by Andrew Kantor. Reproduced by permission.

I f I see one more article about how wonderful alternative energy is compared to oil, I'm gonna flip. Alternative energy sources can be good—very good in fact. And it's pretty obvious that we're going to need them, and that our dependence on oil (foreign or otherwise) is a Bad Thing.

But accepting that does not mean accepting that any kind of alternative energy is by default a good thing.

To be a good thing, it has to have three properties: 1) It has to help reduce our dependence on oil, 2) It has to be no worse for the environment, and 3) It has to be economically practical.

## Alternative Energy Is Not Always Good

Many of the things touted meet one or even two of those criteria. Solar panels, for example. They can reduce our need for oil, at least in certain regions, and they're certainly not bad for the environment.

*A station attendant fills up a vehicle with diesel fuel, a fuel that is more environmentally friendly than either ethanol or electricity.*

But they're prohibitively expensive. If you spend the money to make your home solar-powered, you probably won't recoup your costs for at least 15 years, which approaches the lifespan of the panels.

I realize that these days, taking a moderate position on anything makes you the enemy of everyone who has an extreme view. But green isn't always good, and oil isn't always bad.

Certainly we need to clean up our act big time and find viable sources of alternative energy. Depending on the Saudis—and oil—for our energy needs is stupid.

But we also have to keep in mind that every one of these alternative energy sources comes at a cost, which is something people seem to forget. They hear the phrase "alternative energy" and automatically assume it's got to be good.

And this makes them no better than the people who hear it and think it's a waste of time.

## Ethanol Does Not Help the Environment

Two seemingly "green" technologies that pop up again and again are ethanol and electric cars. Both are touted by well-meaning people as good for the environment and a way to reduce our oil dependence, especially as oil prices continue to rise.

> **FAST FACT**
>
> According to the General Accounting Office, an electric van creates 763 percent more sulfur dioxide emissions than does an efficient gasoline-powered van.

I've written in detail about ethanol before, but it deserves a rehash. The Senate, you see, is considering a bill that would require a doubling of the amount of ethanol mixed with gasoline at the pump. [1]

They say it's about oil dependence and the environment, but it's not. It's about buying votes from farmers by artificially creating demand for crops—ethanol coming, in large part, from corn. But there are a bunch of problems with ethanol. First, it doesn't have as much energy as gasoline, which means it takes about 1.5 gallons of

---

1. In August 2005 an energy bill that contained that provision was signed into law by President Bush.

*Corn is used to produce ethanol, an alternative fuel that critics argue produces more pollution than gasoline.*

ethanol to get you as far as one gallon of gas. Ethanol also requires a lot to produce it—pounds of corn to get a gallon, in fact. And growing corn requires lots of water and fertilizer and pesticide, not to mention the energy required to distill it into ethanol.

And by-products of that distillation include (according to the EPA [Environmental Protection Agency]) acetic acid, carbon monoxide, formaldehyde, and methanol, all of which are pumped into the air. Yum.

It boils down to this: Ethanol sounds good, but the energy required to produce it, and the pollutants it generates, mean it's arguably worse for the environment than gasoline, especially considering the cleanliness of today's engines.

On the other hand, even with the acreage, water, fertilizer, and pesticide, ethanol has one big thing going for it: It's not produced by the Saudis.

## Dirtier than Gasoline

Hearing the un-researched praises heaped on ethanol sets my teeth on edge, but hearing the supposed ecological wonders of electric cars makes me want to bang my head against the desk. (I'm talking about true electric vehicles, not hybrids.)

Electric cars are dirty. In fact, not only are they dirty, they might even be more dirty than their gasoline-powered cousins. People in California love to talk about "zero-emissions vehicles," but people in California seem to be clueless about where electricity comes from. How else can you explain a state that uses more and more of it while not allowing new power plants to be built? . . .

Aside from the few folks who have their roofs covered with solar cells, we get our electricity from generators. Generators are fueled by something—usually a hydrocarbon (coal, oil, diesel) but also by heat generated in nuclear power plants. (There are a few wind farms and geothermal plants as well, but by far we get electricity by burning something.)

In other words, those "zero-emissions" cars are likely coal-burning cars. It's just the coal is burned somewhere else so it looks clean.

It isn't. It's as if the California Greens are covering their eyes—"If I can't see it, it's not happening."

## The Benefits of Gasoline

But it's worse than that. Gasoline is an incredibly efficient way to power a vehicle; a gallon of gas has a lot of energy in it. But when you take that gas (or another fuel) and first use it to make electricity, you waste a nice chunk of that energy, mostly in the form of wasted heat—at the generator, through the transmission lines, etc.

In other words, a gallon of gas may propel your car 25 miles. But the electricity you get from that gallon of gas won't get you nearly as far—so electric cars burn more fuel than gas-powered ones. If our electricity came mostly from nukes, or geothermal, or hydro, or solar, or wind, then an electric car truly would be clean. But for political, technical, and economic reasons, we don't use much of those energy sources. We should, but we don't—that means those electric cars have a dirty past.

Furthermore, today's cars are very, very clean. I'd be willing to bet they're a lot cleaner than coal-burning power plants. And that's not even getting into whatever toxic niceties are in those electric cars' batteries—stuff that will eventually end up in a landfill. And finally, when cars are the polluters, the pollution is spread across all the roads. When it's a power plant, though, all the junk is in one place. Nature is very good at cleaning up when things are not too concentrated, but it takes a lot longer when all the garbage is in one spot.

Being green is good. We've squandered our space program on things like the International Space Money Pit, so we won't be leaving the planet very soon. It's what we've got and we should do better at taking care of it.

But that doesn't mean we should jump on any technology labeled "green" anymore than investors should have jumped on any stock labeled "tech" in the 1990s. We know what happened there.

## EVALUATING THE AUTHORS' ARGUMENTS:

In this pair of viewpoints, Lester R. Brown and Andrew Kantor debate the advantages of alternative-fuel automobiles versus those that run on gasoline. Having read both articles, do you think that alternative-fuel cars will one day replace more traditional vehicles? If so, why? If not, what do you think will be the reason? Explain your answers.

**Viewpoint 3**

# Hydrogen Cars Have a Promising Future

### Nicole Davis

*"A growing hydrogen market can do nothing but help renewable energy."*

In the following viewpoint Nicole Davis discusses the benefits of hydrogen as an alternative fuel for automobiles. According to Davis, hydrogen can help reduce America's energy crisis, decrease pollution, and strengthen the nation's power grid. Although technical and political obstacles must be overcome before hydrogen-powered cars are commonplace, Davis believes hydrogen vehicles have a promising future.

Davis is a New York–based freelance writer.

**AS YOU READ, CONSIDER THE FOLLOWING QUESTIONS:**

1. How much carbon dioxide does the average car release each year, according to Davis?
2. In the author's view what is the paradox of hydrogen-powered cars?
3. What is "distributed generation," as explained by Davis?

At Ford's Sustainable Mobility Technologies Lab in Dearborn, Michigan, where engineers are at work on the latest buzz-phrase in driving—hydrogen fuel cell cars—Mugeeb Ijaz runs down the vital stats on the Ford Focus above him. Suspended on a hydraulic lift, the underbelly of the popular sedan seems no different from the average car, except for the black metal box fastened to its middle. In place of the gas tank, explains Ijaz, a supervisor for the fuel cells program at Ford, there is a stack of fuel cells. Instead of gas, this

*An attendee at the 2004 National Clean Cities Conference and Expo has a look at a Ford Focus hydrogen fuel cell electric car.*

prototype, like dozens of others in development around Detroit, runs on hydrogen. Yet the most salient fact about this Focus is what it doesn't do: While the average car releases roughly six tons (5.4 metric tons) of carbon dioxide into the air each year, a hydrogen fuel cell car emits zero pollutants.

Hydrogen can be used in an internal combustion engine. But a fuel cell car—essentially an electric car that uses the cells as a catalyst to convert hydrogen and oxygen into electricity—emits only heat and water vapor. For the environmentally conscious and those anxious over energy security, such benign byproducts could either be a red herring, or a real breakthrough.

## Fueling a Hydrogen Car

Louis Paspal, an engineer with the automaker for the past 12 years, has seen alternatives like electric vehicles come and go in response to public demand for better fuel economy and emissions. "Hydrogen," he says, "is the one that's going to work."

Dressed in blue coveralls, he stood beside the hydrogen "gas" station, ready to fill up one of Ford's fuel cell cars. Paspal and his col-

*A technician works on a low-emission hydrogen car. Hydrogen-powered cars typically generate fewer emissions than gasoline-powered cars.*

*A commuter pumps hydrogen fuel at a gas station in Washington, D.C., the first station in the United States to offer both hydrogen and gasoline.*

league, Ron Gillard, first asked onlookers to stand behind a yellow safety bar a few feet from the car (a precautionary measure for now, explained Paspal). Before filling up, he affixed a plug-like device to the tank for a pressure check. (This step will ultimately be eliminated, Gillard offered, when an electronic sensor automatically reads the tank's pressure.) Finally came the nozzle—bearing a close resemblance to a ray gun—that Gillard used to "pump" the odorless, invisible hydrogen. The entire process will be streamlined in time, but the simple act of refueling provides a glimpse of the complicated switch to a new fuel.

## Obstacles to Hydrogen

Other obstacles include the public's fear of hydrogen, both real and perceived, that need to be assuaged. Even if hydrogen was not the cause for the 1937 *Hindenburg* disaster[1] (scientists now argue it was due to the explosive paint on the zeppelin's exterior), it sticks out in people's minds as a compelling reason to stay away from the element. Education, Ijaz explained earlier, is just one multi-million-dollar line item in the United States Department of Energy's (DOE) budget for hydrogen car research and development.

1. A zeppelin called the *Hindenburg* exploded, killing thirty-six people.

*A test car is filled with liquid hydrogen fuel at a solar-powered filling station in Germany.*

The infrastructure needed to fuel an entire nation of hydrogen-powered cars is another healthy slice of the projected pie chart. While General Motors would like to sell a million hydrogen cars a year by the middle of the next decade, DOE officials expect only to have completed research into implementing the new fuel by 2015. Getting hydrogen cars on the road and hydrogen in filling stations—comparable to the network that now fuels the 200 million gas-powered cars today—would be on the order of 20 to 50 years. That is, if hydrogen turns out to be the means to cleaner-running cars. Ford shies away from concrete predictions. "Who knows," says Phil Chizek, marketing and sales manager of Ford's fuel cell program. "In ten years this may not be the answer. But the truth is, you have to spend some money on advance development. That's what the space program did," Chizek points out. "Look at how many Apollo missions there were."

But there's a paradox: To tap into this zero-emissions energy source, high emissions fuels like coal and gas continue to be the cheapest, at least in economic terms, and most common means to separate hydrogen from the naturally occurring substances it's found in, such as water and gas. . . .

## An Answer to Blackouts

The problem that hydrogen may be most fit to solve in the near future has nothing to do with cars. Instead, it could be a viable solution to the nation's overburdened power grid.

While New York City was in the dark during the largest blackout in U.S. history [in August 2003], a police station in Central Park kept its electrical power flowing with the fuel-cell stack it uses to operate, even when the power's on. And in Ontario, Canada, Stuart Energy weathered the power outage with the air conditioning running, creating buzz for hydrogen power in the process. The Canadian company makes electrolytic stations, or generators that extract hydrogen from water. Naturally, it had a backup supply of hydrogen power—but never had a real life application for it until the blackout.

CEO Jon Slangerup says he was in a meeting when the lights blinked off, then came back on. He mistook the outage for a power surge, but when his meeting ended an hour later, Slangerup says, "I came out to find . . . that entire Eastern region was out. And this system we'd built conceptually popped on in eight seconds. We didn't lose any time in our business."

Stuart Energy plans to capitalize on the notion of "distributed generation" that's gained currency since the blackout. The idea loosely entails a dispersed system of individual, small-scale power stations that could operate in conjunction with the grid. In Stuart Energy's model, solar energy panels would fuel the electrolyzing process. The resulting hydrogen

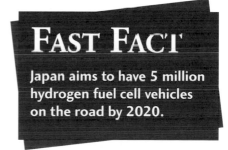

**FAST FACT**

Japan aims to have 5 million hydrogen fuel cell vehicles on the road by 2020.

would then generate enough electricity to power a home and fuel the cars in the garage. The initial cost for such a system to individual homeowners would approach U.S. $25,000, a relatively exorbitant sum. But once running, solar-powered hydrogen systems would eliminate home and car owners' monthly electric bill and gas charges.

## Hydrogen Can Work with Other Energies

Not to mention personal contributions to the greenhouse effect. Hydrogen takes energy to produce. But once created, hydrogen can store energy for future use, making it the perfect partner to capture intermittent power generated by wind and solar energy. Such a future is a long way off, but William Hoagland, former hydrogen program manager for the DOE's National Renewable Energy Laboratory agrees that weaknesses in the power grid may be the catalyst to kick-start the hydrogen economy. Even if we use fossil fuels for the next century to create it, ultimately, says Hoagland, "A growing hydrogen market can do nothing but help renewable energy."

"Our big problem is not making the fuel cell cars or the hydrogen. It's the infrastructure," he says. "If there were a market today for large amounts of hydrogen, you would see infrastructure problems change. It's a chicken and egg problem."

With the country's energy anxieties heightened, it may seem that stationary fuel cell power will be first to drive the hydrogen market. But cars have a history of predating the systems that support them—namely gas stations and a network of paved roads. One hundred years ago, early automobile owners waited nearly a decade before either appeared to make driving easier and cars cheaper. Once that infrastructure took shape, cars, initially called playthings of the rich, lost their derisive nickname as well.

## EVALUATING THE AUTHOR'S ARGUMENTS:

Nicole Davis writes that Americans must learn that hydrogen is not dangerous so they can embrace it as an energy source. Assuming her view is accurate, what steps would you take to teach people about the benefits of hydrogen? Use information from the viewpoint to support your answer.

# Hydrogen Cars
# Are Not Viable

### Joseph Romm

*"Hydrogen cars are likely to remain inferior to the best gasoline-electric hybrid vehicles."*

Hydrogen-powered cars cannot solve America's energy problems, Joseph Romm argues in the following viewpoint. Hydrogen cars run by converting hydrogen and oxygen into electricity and heat. But Romm explains they are not ready for commercial use because they are too expensive and require serious technological breakthroughs. He also argues that hydrogen-run cars are not better for the environment than traditional vehicles.

Romm was the acting assistant secretary of energy for energy efficiency and renewable energy during the Clinton administration. He is also the author of *The Hype About Hydrogen: Fact and Fiction in the Race to Save the Climate.*

## AS YOU READ, CONSIDER THE FOLLOWING QUESTIONS:

1. What are the "two pillars" of a hydrogen economy, as explained by the author?
2. According to Romm, how much more expensive are transportation fuel cells compared to internal combustion engines?
3. How long does Romm think it will take before hydrogen cars can help reduce global warming?

Hydrogen and fuel-cell cars are being mightily promoted. The U.S. Department of Energy has made them the central focus of its clean energy efforts. The state of California has said it will in the next few years build a "hydrogen highway," with hydrogen fueling stations every 20 miles along major highways. General Motors is spending more than a quarter of its research budget on fuel-cell vehicles and Larry Burns, GM's vice president for R&D [research and development] and planning, said in February [2004] that the company will have a commercially viable fuel-cell vehicle by 2010.

Yet for all this hype, hydrogen cars are likely to remain inferior to the best gasoline-electric hybrid vehicles such as the Toyota Prius in virtually every respect—cost, range, annual fueling bill, convenience, safety—through at least 2030. The Prius will even have lower overall emissions of many pollutants than cars running on the hydrogen that is likely to be available at fueling stations for the foreseeable future. And a premature push toward hydrogen cars would undermine efforts to reduce the heat-trapping carbon dioxide emissions that cause global climate change.

## Not Yet Practical

For hydrogen cars to become both practical from a consumer's perspective and desirable from an environmental perspective will require at least three major technology breakthroughs. In addition, the nation will have to shift its energy policy dramatically toward renewable energy sources such as wind and solar.

Don't get me wrong. I am a strong proponent of hydrogen as a possible fuel for the future. In fact, I helped oversee the Department of Energy's program for clean energy, including hydrogen, for much of the 1990s—during which time we increased funding for hydrogen technologies tenfold. I believe that continued research into hydrogen remains important because of its potential to provide a pollution-free substitute for oil post-2030. But going beyond R&D at this point to actually building the hydrogen infrastructure—as many advocate—is both unjustified and unwise. As Peter Flynn, an engineering professor at the University of Alberta, concluded in a 2002 study of the effort to commercialize natural gas vehicles:

"Exaggerated claims have damaged the credibility of alternate transportation fuels, and have retarded acceptance, especially by large commercial purchasers."

Let's briefly look at why hydrogen cars are still a long way from making sense.

## An Expensive Energy

In a "hydrogen economy," the main energy carrier would be hydrogen that is produced from pollution-free sources of energy. This goal rests on two pillars: a pollution-free source for the hydrogen and a device for cleanly converting this hydrogen into useful energy (the fuel cell).

Hydrogen is not a readily accessible energy source like coal or wind. It is bound up tightly in molecules like water ($H_2O$) and natural gas (primarily composed of methane, or $CH_4$) so it is expensive and energy-intensive to extract and purify. More than 95 percent of U.S. hydrogen is produced from natural gas today because that is the cheapest method. Yet delivering hydrogen from natural gas to the tank of a

*One drawback of hydrogen cars is their limited range. The car shown here can only travel approximately forty-seven miles before refueling.*

fuel-cell car in usable form costs four times as much as gasoline with an equivalent amount of energy. Hydrogen from pollution-free sources, such as renewables, is even more expensive. A hydrogen infrastructure built around existing or near-commercial technologies would cost more than $600 billion, according to the most comprehensive study done, by the Argonne National Laboratory.

Fuel cells are small, modular, electrochemical devices, similar to batteries, but which can be continuously fueled. A fuel cell takes in hydrogen and oxygen and puts out electricity and heat; its only "emissions" are water. This sounds like an energy panacea—but today, more

than 160 years after the first fuel cell was built, and after more than $15 billion in public and private spending, fuel-cell technology still has not achieved major commercial success.

## Technical Difficulties

The technical challenges are enormous. In September 2003, a U.S. Department of Energy panel on basic research needs for the hydrogen economy, chaired by MIT [Massachusetts Institute of Technology] professor of physics and electrical engineering Mildred Dresselhaus, reported that transportation fuel cells are 100 times more expensive than internal combustion engines. The most mature hydrogen storage systems—using ultrahigh pressure—contain seven to 10 times less energy per unit volume than gasoline, and require a significant amount of compression energy. [In February 2004] a prestigious National Academy of Sciences panel con-

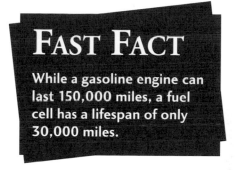

**FAST FACT**

While a gasoline engine can last 150,000 miles, a fuel cell has a lifespan of only 30,000 miles.

cluded that such storage has "little promise of long-term practicality." And a report published [in March 2004] by the American Physical Society concluded that "a new material must be discovered" to solve the storage problem.

The Department of Energy panel noted that the cost of producing hydrogen would have to be reduced by a factor of four to make hydrogen economically competitive with today's fossil fuels. Major advances would also be required in hydrogen infrastructure and safety. The panel concluded that these gaps "cannot be bridged by incremental advances of the present state of the art," but instead require "revolutionary conceptual breakthroughs."

If this sounds like it will be a long time before we see a commercially viable product in the marketplace, that should be no surprise.

Breakthroughs that revolutionize energy technology are rare. It has taken wind power and solar power each about 20 years to see a tenfold decline in prices, after major government and private-sector investments in R&D and deployment—and they still account for well under one percent of U.S. electricity generation.

*Hydrogen-powered cars, such as this concept vehicle pictured at a trade show, are years away from becoming a common sight on the world's roadways.*

## The Drawbacks of Hydrogen Cars

Alternative fuel vehicles (AFVs) are a greater challenge, because they must overcome a trillion-dollar investment in the gasoline fueling infrastructure. Two major efforts to commercialize AFVs in the past two decades—electric vehicles and natural gas vehicles—both failed, even though electricity and natural gas are widely available and inexpensive. Hydrogen, by contrast, is hardly available anywhere and is relatively expensive. Our cars and our fueling infrastructure are designed around liquid fuels, which have high energy densities and are easier to handle than diffuse gases like hydrogen.

Based on my discussions with experts around the country, I think it unlikely that hydrogen cars will achieve even a five percent market share by 2030. But we shouldn't be in a hurry to deploy hydrogen cars.

It is a popular misconception that hydrogen is inherently good for the environment. But in fact, hydrogen is no greener than the energy sources used to produce it. As the National Academy panel noted, "It is highly likely that fossil fuels will be the principal sources of hydrogen for several decades." Any premature push toward hydrogen cars would inevitably mean the hydrogen would come from the cheapest source today, natural gas. Yet, given the constraints on the North American gas supply, we would just be trading imported gas for imported oil.

More important, a fuel-cell car running on hydrogen derived from natural gas offers no significant greenhouse gas savings compared to running advanced hybrid vehicles on oil—as a 2003 MIT study concluded. The best new hybrids have sharply reduced their fuel consumption and hence greenhouse gas emissions. Running on low-sulfur gasoline, the 2004 Prius produces 90 percent less tailpipe emissions than the average new car. The least expensive hydrogen, however, is dirty. Based on the hydrogen fueling stations Royal Dutch/Shell has proposed to build, the total emissions of nitrogen oxides from a fuel-cell vehicle would be triple that of the best new cars. . . .

## Not a Plausible Solution

The U.S. Congress . . . won't pass legislation requiring even 10 percent of electricity in 2020 to be from renewables. This means that hydrogen cars will have no real value as a global warming strategy until after 2030. A 2004 analysis by Pacific Northwest National Laboratory concluded that even with technology breakthroughs and a big push on reducing carbon dioxide emissions, "hydrogen doesn't penetrate the transportation sector in a major way until after 2035."

Right now, delivering renewable hydrogen to a car in usable form is prohibitively expensive—equivalent to gasoline at $6 to $10 a gallon. We need a major breakthrough in $CO_2$-neutral hydrogen production, along with significant leaps forward in fuel cells and hydrogen storage, before hydrogen cars will be plausible competitors.

**EVALUATING THE AUTHORS' ARGUMENTS:**

Authors Nicole Davis and Joseph Romm both acknowledge that hydrogen-powered automobiles are not yet commercially viable. However, they disagree on whether hydrogen can eventually be a useful source of energy. Whose conclusion do you find more convincing and why?

# Glossary

**alternative fuel:** Transportation fuel created from natural gas or from organic materials.

**biodiesel:** A renewable fuel that is created from animal fat or vegetable oils and can be used in engines.

**biofuel:** Fuel produced from organic matter.

**emissions:** Substances, such as pollutants or greenhouse gases, which are released into the air, soil, or water.

**ethanol:** An alternative automobile fuel produced from grain or corn.

**fossil fuels:** Fuels formed from decayed animals and plants, in particular coal, oil, and natural gas.

**fuel cells:** Devices that convert hydrogen fuel into electricity.

**fusion:** The process by which nuclear energy is created, caused when nuclei from atoms combine into a larger nucleus.

**global warming:** A gradual increase in the earth's temperature, which many people speculate is caused by the burning of **fossil fuels**.

**hybrid engines:** Engines that combine two fuels, typically gasoline and electric batteries.

**internal combustion engine:** An engine in which the combustion of fuel occurs inside the engine.

**megawatt-hour:** A measurement of energy; the amount of megawatts (1 million watts) generated in one hour.

**photovoltaic:** Converting sunlight into electricity; a synonym for "solar electric."

**renewable energy:** Energy that does not come from **fossil fuels** and therefore can be constantly replenished. Examples include wind energy, solar energy, and hydroelectric power.

**wind turbines:** A machine that converts the kinetic energy (energy associated with motion) in wind into mechanical energy.

Editor's Note: These facts can be used in reports or papers to reinforce or add credibility when making important points or claims.

## Oil and Energy Consumption

- According to the Energy Information Administration, the average American consumes six times more energy than the world average.
- The typical U.S. family spends $1,500 per year on utility bills.
- Almost two-thirds of the oil used in the United States is imported.
- According to the U.S. National Intelligence Council, 80 percent of the world's oil has yet to be extracted from the planet.
- According to the Solar Energy Institute, world energy consumption is expected to rise between 40 and 50 percent by 2010. Carbon dioxide emissions will increase by 50 to 60 percent.
- The United States releases 23 percent of the world's energy-related carbon emissions. The activities of the average American family produce twenty-three thousand pounds of carbon dioxide each year.
- There are more than 500,000 oil-producing wells in the United States, but most of them produce only a few barrels of oil per day.
- In 2003, according to the Energy Information Administration, the top oil producing areas in the United States were the Gulf of Mexico (1.6 million barrels per day) and Texas onshore (1.1 million barrels per day).
- According to the *CIA World Factbook*, Americans consume 3.66 trillion kilowatts of electricity per year and 19.65 million barrels of oil each day. However, the United States produces only 7.8 million barrels per day.
- The production of oil has reached its peak or begun to decline in thirty-three of the forty-eight largest producers, including in six of the eleven members of the Organization of Petroleum Exporting Countries.
- Global energy consumption is 130 times greater than it was prior to the Industrial Revolution.

- The United States accounts for one-fourth of global oil consumption.

## Solar and Wind Energy

- According to the Union of Concerned Scientists, the amount of sunlight that reaches the United States equals five hundred times America's annual energy demands.
- There are more than one-quarter million solar homes in the United States.
- According to the European Wind Energy Association, the number of people employed in the wind energy industry in Europe has nearly tripled since 1998, from twenty-five thousand employees to seventy-two thousand employees.
- The world's largest wind farm produces 278.2 megawatts of electricity in a year, which can supply electricity to about seventy-two thousand homes, according to the American Wind Energy Association.
- Winds in the United States contain energy equivalent to forty times the amount used by Americans, according to the Union of Concerned Scientists.
- Solar water heaters are common in some countries that receive a lot of sunlight. All new homes and apartments in Israel are required to use solar energy to heat water, and more than 90 percent of the homes in Cyprus have solar water heaters.
- The winds in North Dakota could generate sufficient power to meet more than one-quarter of U.S. electricity demand, according to the American Wind Energy Association.
- In 2002 wind farms provided electricity for 40 million Europeans.
- Wind energy currently generates only 0.1 percent of America's electricity. In California, 1 percent of electricity is created by wind; that percentage could increase to 5 percent by 2020.

## Nuclear Energy

- Atoms were first used to produce electric power in December 1951.
- Approximately 20 percent of the electricity generated in the United States comes from nuclear power.
- According to the Nuclear Energy Institute, as of 2003 nuclear power plants created 16 percent of the world's electricity. The three nations that receive the largest amounts of their electricity from nuclear ener-

gy are Lithuania (79.9 percent), France (77.7 percent) and Slovakia (57.4 percent).

- According to the Nuclear Energy Institute, 442 nuclear plants in thirty-one nations are used to generate electricity.
- The first full-scale nuclear power plant, located in Shippingport, Pennsylvania, went into service on December 2, 1957. At full power it could generate sixty megawatts of electricity.
- One hundred three commercial nuclear power plants in thirty-one states produce electricity in the United States.
- As of 2005, the average plant was twenty-four years old.
- The Palo Verde Nuclear Generating Station in Arizona produces more energy annually than any other U.S. power plant, including those powered by oil and natural gas.
- Vermont receives 74 percent of its electricity from nuclear power, more than any other state. New Jersey, South Carolina, Illinois, and Connecticut garner more than half of their electricity from nuclear energy.
- Radioactive waste from nuclear reactors must be stored for at least 300,000 years.
- According to the U.S. Bureau of Labor Statistics, working at a nuclear power plant is safer than working in real estate or finance.

## Alternative-Fuel Automobiles

- Americans own one-third of the world's automobiles, but comprise less than 5 percent of the world's population.
- The average American uses five hundred gallons of gasoline each year.
- According to *OnEarth* magazine, Americans drive 60 percent more miles than British, French, German, Swedish, Japanese, Canadian, and Mexican drivers combined.
- The United States produced 2.81 billion gallons of ethanol in 2003.
- According to the Hybrid Car Organization, midsized hybrid cars such as the Toyota Prius and Honda Insight produce 3.5 tons of greenhouse gas emissions, approximately half the amount of similar-sized gasoline-powered vehicles.
- One bushel of soybeans can produce 1.4 gallons of biodiesel, according to the Iowa Department of Agriculture and Land Stewardship.

# Organizations to Contact

**American Council for an Energy-Efficient Economy**
1001 Connecticut Ave. NW, Suite 801, Washington, DC 20036
(202) 429-8873
e-mail: info@aceee.org
Web site: www.aceee.org

The American Council for an Energy-Efficient Economy is a non-profit organization interested in energy efficiency. The council assesses energy policy, works with businesses and public interest groups, and educates businesses and consumers.

**American Petroleum Institute**
1220 L St. NW, Washington, DC 20005
(202) 682-8000
Web site: www.api.org

The American Petroleum Institute represents America's petroleum industry. It lobbies, conducts research, and sets technical standards for the petroleum industry.

**American Solar Energy Society**
2400 Central Ave., Suite A, Boulder, CO 80301
(303) 443-3130
e-mail: ases@ases.org
Web site: www.ases.org

The American Solar Energy Society is a nonprofit organization that promotes the widespread use of solar energy.

**American Wind Energy Association (AWEA)**
1101 Fourteenth St. NW, 12th Fl., Washington, DC 20005
(202) 383-2500
e-mail: windmail@awea.org
Web site: www.awea.org

The American Wind Energy Association is a national trade association that represents utilities, wind power plant developers, and other participants in the wind industry. AWEA provides information on such topics as wind energy projects and policy developments related to wind and other types of renewable energy.

## Canadian Association for Renewable Energies
435 Brennan, Ottawa, ON K1Z 6J9 Canada
(613) 728-0822
e-mail: eggertson@renewables.ca
Web site: www.renewables.ca

The Canadian Association for Renewable Energies is a not-for-profit organization that promotes renewable sources of energy. It provides daily updates on renewable energy to members and subscribers.

## Competitive Enterprise Institute (CEI)
1001 Connecticut Ave. NW, Suite 1250, Washington, DC 20036
(202) 331-1010
e-mail: info@cei.org
Web site: www.cei.org

CEI is a nonprofit public policy organization dedicated to the principles of free enterprise and limited government. The institute believes private incentives and property rights, rather than government regulations, are the best way to protect the environment.

## National Resources Defense Council (NRDC)
40 W. Twentieth St., New York, NY 10011
(212) 727-2700
e-mail: nrdcinfo@nrdc.org
Web site: www.nrdc.org

The NRDC is a nonprofit organization that uses laws and science to protect the environment. It believes that one of the best ways people can fight water pollution and global warming is by becoming more energy efficient and by using wind and solar power.

## Nuclear Energy Institute
1776 I St. NW, Suite 400, Washington, DC 20006-3708
(202) 739-8000
e-mail: webmaster@nei.org
Web site: www.nei.org

The Nuclear Energy Institute is the policy organization of the nuclear energy and technologies industry. Its goal is the creation of policies that encourage the use of nuclear energy throughout the world.

## Nuclear Information and Resource Service (NIRS)
1424 Sixteenth St. NW, #404, Washington, DC 20036
(202) 328-0002
e-mail: nirsnet@nirs.org
Web site: www.nirs.org

The Nuclear Information and Resource Service works to create a nuclear-free planet. NIRS provides information to people who are concerned about issues such as radioactive waste and nuclear power.

## Political Economy Research Center (PERC)
2048 Analysis Dr., Suite A, Bozeman, MT, 59718
(406) 587-9591
e-mail: perc@perc.org
Web site: www.perc.org

PERC is a nonprofit research and educational organization that seeks market-oriented solutions to environmental problems. One of the problems addressed by PERC is America's energy supply. The center holds a variety of conferences and provides environmental educational material.

## Union of Concerned Scientists (UCS)
2 Brattle Square, Cambridge, MA 02238-9105
(617) 547-5552
Web site: www.ucsusa.org

The Union of Concerned Scientists is an organization of scientists and other citizens concerned about nuclear energy and the impact of advanced technology on society. The UCS conducts independent research and testifies at congressional and regulatory hearings.

## U.S. Department of Energy
1000 Independence Ave. SW, Washington, DC 20585
(800) 342-5363
Web site: www.doe.gov

The U.S. Department of Energy has several missions, including promoting the delivery of reliable and environmentally sound sources of energy. Information on energy efficiency and traditional and alternative sources of energy is available on the site.

## Worldwatch Institute
1776 Massachusetts Ave. NW, Washington, DC 20036-1904
(202) 452-1999
e-mail: worldwatch@worldwatch.org
Web site: www.worldwatch.org

Worldwatch is a nonprofit public policy research organization dedicated to informing the public and policy makers about emerging global problems and trends and the complex links between the environment and the world economy.

# For Further Reading

## Books

Asmus, Peter, *Reaping the Wind: How Mechanical Wizards, Visionaries, and Profiteers Helped Shape Our Energy Future.* Washington, DC: Island Press, 2001. A journalist details the history of wind power in the United States.

Berinstein, Paula, *Alternative Energy: Facts, Statistics, and Issues.* Westport, CT: Oryx Press, 2001. An overview of the history of energy use and analyses of the major types of alternative energy, such as wind and solar.

Deffeyes, Kenneth S., *Hubbert's Peak: The Impending World Oil Shortage.* Princeton, NJ: Princeton University Press, 2001. A former geologist argues that the decline in global oil production could lead to a world-wide recession.

Ewing, Rex A., *Power with Nature: Solar and Wind Energy Demystified.* Masonville, CO: PixyJack Press, 2003. The author explains how people can use solar and wind energy in their homes.

Fanchi, John R., *Energy in the 21st Century.* Hackensack, NJ: World Scientific, 2005. Looks at different types of energy and forecasts the future of energy.

Gipe, Paul, *Wind Power: Renewable Energy for Home, Farm, and Business.* White River Junction, VT: Chelsea Green, 2004. A useful reference for people who want to utilize wind technology, providing information on the financial and energy savings.

Heinberg, Richard, *The Party's Over: Oil, War, and the Fate of Industrial Societies.* Gabriola, BC: New Society, 2003. A look at why the oil supply is depleting and how that could lead to resource wars in South America, the Middle East, and Central Asia.

Hoffmann, Peter, *Tomorrow's Energy: Hydrogen, Fuel Cells, and the Prospects for a Cleaner Planet.* Cambridge, MA: MIT Press, 2001. The author details the history of hydrogen energy and the benefits of a hydrogen-based economy.

Hostetter, Martha, ed. *Energy Policy.* New York: H.W. Wilson, 2002. An anthology of articles that address energy policy and alternative fuels.

Kryza, Frank, *The Power of Light: The Epic Story of Man's Quest to Harness the Sun.* New York: McGraw-Hill, 2003. An expert in solar energy explores the history of solar energy, from the mid-nineteenth century through modern times.

Kunstler, James Howard, *The Long Emergency.* New York: Atlantic Monthly Press, 2005. The author argues that the decline in global oil production will drastically change American culture.

Mannwell, J.F., J.G. McGowan, and A.L. Rogers, *Wind Energy Explained: Theory, Design, and Application.* New York: Wiley, 2002. Explores the history of wind energy, wind turbines, and the economic and environmental effects of wind energy systems.

Perlin, John, *From Space to Earth: The Story of Solar Electricity.* Cambridge, MA: Harvard University Press, 2002. Explores the history of solar power, with an emphasis on the effects of solar electricity on the developing world.

Roberts, Paul, *The End of Oil: On the Edge of a Perilous New World.* Boston: Houghton Mifflin, 2004. The author explores the global depletion of oil and how that is changing society.

Romm, Joseph J., *The Hype About Hydrogen: Fact and Fiction in the Race to Save the Climate.* Washington, DC: Island Press, 2004. An examination of hydrogen and fuel cell technologies and why it will be difficult to transition to a hydrogen economy.

Sperling, Daniel, and James S. Canon, eds., *The Hydrogen Energy Transition: Moving Toward the Post Petroleum Age in Transportation.* Boston: Elsevier, 2004. Analyzes whether a transition to hydrogen power can occur and what steps need to be taken if such a transition is possible.

Williams, Laurence O., *An End to Global Warming.* Boston: Pergamon, 2002. The author argues that society must stop using fossil fuels and turn to alternative energy if it wants to protect the environment.

## Periodicals

Barlett, Donald L., and James B. Steele, "The U.S. Is Running Out of Energy," *Time,* July 21, 2003.

Bivens, Matt, "Fighting for America's Energy Independence," *Nation,* April 15, 2002.

Brown, Lester R., "Turning On: Renewable Energy," *Mother Earth News,* April/May 2004.

Chandler, David, "America Steels Itself to Take the Nuclear Plunge," *New Scientist,* August 9, 2003.

Drum, Kevin, "Crude Awakening" *Washington Monthly,* June 2005.

*Economist,* "Why the Future Is Hybrid," December 4, 2004.

Edgens, Jefferson G., "What Energy Policy?" *World & I,* November 2003.

Fairley, Peter, "Solar-Cell Rollout," *Technology Review,* July/August 2004.

Fishman, Ted C., "Cars That Guzzle Grass," *New York Times Magazine,* September 25, 2005.

Livingston, Doug, and Scott Hollis, "Simpler Solar Power," *Mother Earth News,* June/July 2005.

McMillen, Margot Ford, "Energy Is More than Oil," *Progressive Populist,* April 15, 2005.

Moore, Stephen, "Bad Surge," *National Review,* May 23, 2005.

Mouawad, Jad, and Matthew L. Wald, "The Oil Uproar That Isn't," *New York Times,* July 12, 2005.

Newman, Richard J., "Invasion of the Green Machines," *U.S. News & World Report,* May 9, 2005.

Olson, Robert L., "The Promise and Pitfalls of Hydrogen Energy," *Futurist,* July/August 2003.

Randerson, James, "The Clean Green Energy Dream," *New Scientist,* August 16, 2003.

Reder, Alan, "Here Comes the Sun," *OnEarth,* Winter 2004.

Tompkins, Joshua, "Wind Power Reconsidered," *Popular Science,* November 1, 2004.

## Web Resources

**ClimateArk** (www.climateark.org). This Web site is a portal and search engine that promotes public policy related to global climate change and provides links to Web sites and news articles about alternative energy.

**Energy Education Resources** (www.eia.doe.gov/bookshelf/eer/kiddiet oc.html). An online publication of the National Energy Information

Center (NEIC), a service of the Energy Information Administration (EIA), that provides links to and information on dozens of energy-related organizations.

**Energy Information Portal** (www.eere.energy.gov). Operated by the U.S. Department of Energy, the portal is a gateway to numerous documents and Web sites on renewable energy and energy efficiency.

**Environmental News Network** (www.enn.com). An online environmental news source, including links to articles on alternative energy.

**Natural Resources and Environment** (www.usda.gov). This Web site provides information on the U.S. Department of Agriculture's energy policies.

# Index

sources, 95–96
cost of producing, 99–101
obstacles to, 93–94

Ijaz, Mugeeb, 91, 93

*Journal of Epidemiology and
Community Health,* 52

Kantor, Andrew, 84
Kuntsler, James Howard, 17

Lieberman, Ben, 72
Lovins, Hunter, 36
Luther, Joachim, 32

McKibben, Bill, 55

National Academy of Sciences, 39,
53–54, 101
National Energy Act (1978), 11
National Renewable Energy
Laboratory, 34
National Wind Resource Inventory,
81
nuclear power, 45, 46, 48
risks of, 52–54
Nuclear Regulatory Commission
(NRC), 50, 53
nuclear waste management, 46–47
Nuclear Waste Policy Act (1982),
46

oil, 27
decline in production of, 18–19,
21–22
may have nonfossil source,
19–20, 25–26
price of, 12–13, 31, 39

Organization of Petroleum Exporting
Countries (OPEC), 11, 19

Pacific Northwest National
Laboratory, 103
Paspal, Louis, 92
Pinkerton, Roger, 26
pollution, 46
Prius (hybrid vehicle), 40, 103

Reagan, Ronald, 12, 76
Reagan administration, 30–31
Roberts, Paul, 29
Romm, Joseph, 97

Sierra Club, 64
Slangerup, Jon, 95
Smith, Charles, 11–12
Solar Decathalon, 73
solar energy, 11, 12
advances by Germany and Japan
in, 32–33
cost of, 75, 86
federal subsidies for, 31–32, 76
increase in demand for, 69, 71
surveys, on support for nuclear
power, 46

Ulmishek, Gregory, 28
United States, 19, 37
is losing technological edge, 30–31

wind energy, 11–12, 35, 58, 83
as danger to wildlife, 63–64
limitations of, 61–63
reduction in cost of, 81–82

Yucca Mountain site, 46, 47

zero net-energy homes, 69–70

# Picture Credits

Cover: Martin Bond/Photo Researchers, Inc.
Maury Aaseng, 68
AFP/Getty Images, 20, 47, 58, 77, 99
AP/Wide World Photos, 33, 51, 82
Aurora/Getty Images, 45
Martin Bond/Photo Researchers, Inc., 42, 94
Dennis Brack/Landov, 93
Michael Caronna/Bloomberg News/Landov, 102
Getty Images, 13, 14, 24, 31, 37, 40, 62, 73, 74, 79, 85, 87, 91
Al Golub/UPI/Landov, 38
Brian Harris/Alamy, 56

David Halpern/SPL/Photo Researchers, 25
Lester Lefkowitz/CORBIS, 21, 61
Newhouse News Service/Landov, 52
Albert Olive/EPA/Landov, 70
Katy Raddatz/CORBIS, 67
Roger Ressmeyer/CORBIS, 44
Pete Saloutos/CORBIS, 16
Volker Steger/Photo Researchers, Inc., 92
Time Life Pictures/Getty Images, 12
Victor Habbick Visions, 18, 27, 75
Ingo Wagner/EPA/Landov, 57

# About the Editor

San Diego resident Laura K. Egendorf received her BA in English from Wesleyan University. A book editor at Greenhaven Press since 1997, she is especially interested in projects that explore free speech or popular culture. When she is not working, her interests include sports, food, and music.